Routledge Revivals

Massacre at Amritsar

First published in 1963, *Massacre at Amritsar* recreates the terrible scene of the Jallianwala Bagh from the stories of eyewitnesses and survivors. General Dyer's action at Amritsar on April 13, 1919, flared up into one of the most heated political and moral controversies of 20th century. Was he right in firing without warning on the group which had gathered in defiance of his orders? And in continuing to fire after they had started to disperse? Did he thereby save Punjab from worse bloodshed, and all India, perhaps, from a second Mutiny? Or did he commit a cold-blooded, purposeless massacre, for which no excuse was possible?

The Army, which had condoned his act on his first explanation, could not stomach his arrogant replies at the enquiry. The Government of India described Dyer's act as 'monstrous.' And perhaps more than any other single factor the massacre consolidated Indian opinion behind the campaign for independence. Yet a large section of the British public backed Dyer; a huge subscription was raised for him, and the House of Lords exonerated him. This book examines the circumstances that led up to the massacre and the deplorable actions that followed it and offers a new solution to the enigma of Dyer's mind, making it an important read for students of history, South Asian studies, area studies and for the people of any erstwhile colonized nation.

Massacre at Amritsar

Rupert Furneaux

Routledge
Taylor & Francis Group

First published in 1963
by George Allen & Unwin Ltd

This edition first published in 2022 by Routledge
4 Park Square, Milton Park, Abingdon, Oxon, OX14 4RN
and by Routledge
605 Third Avenue, New York, NY 10017

Routledge is an imprint of the Taylor & Francis Group, an informa business

© Rupert Furneaux, 1963

All rights reserved. No part of this book may be reprinted or reproduced or utilised in any form or by any electronic, mechanical, or other means, now known or hereafter invented, including photocopying and recording, or in any information storage or retrieval system, without permission in writing from the publishers.

Publisher's Note
The publisher has gone to great lengths to ensure the quality of this reprint but points out that some imperfections in the original copies may be apparent.

Disclaimer
The publisher has made every effort to trace copyright holders and welcomes correspondence from those they have been unable to contact.

A Library of Congress record exists under LCCN: 66037035

ISBN: 978-1-032-33435-6 (hbk)
ISBN: 978-1-003-31966-5 (ebk)
ISBN: 978-1-032-33436-3 (pbk)

Book DOI 10.4324/9781003319665

MASSACRE AT AMRITSAR

by the same author

THE FIRST WAR CORRESPONDENT
(William Howard Russell of *The Times*)

THE OTHER SIDE OF THE STORY

FACT, FAKE OR FABLE?

THE MAN BEHIND THE MASK

MYTH AND MYSTERY

FAMOUS CRIMINAL CASES I-VII

THE MEDICAL MURDERER

THE SIEGE OF PLEVNA (In U.S.A., THE BREAKFAST WAR)

TRIED BY THEIR PEERS

LEGEND AND REALITY

TOBIAS FURNEAUX, CIRCUMNAVIGATOR

THE TWO STRANGLERS OF RILLINGTON PLACE

THE WORLD'S STRANGEST MYSTERIES

CRIME DOCUMENTARIES:
    1 GUENTHER PODOLA
    2 ROBERT HOOLHOUSE
    3 THE MURDER OF LORD ERROLL
    4 MICHAEL DAVIES

THE ZULU WAR (GREAT BATTLES OF HISTORY)

COURTROOM, USA, I, II

THE MYSTERY OF THE EMPTY TOMB

THEY DIED BY A GUN

Brigadier-General R. E. H. Dyer

MASSACRE
AT
AMRITSAR

BY
RUPERT FURNEAUX

ILLUSTRATED

London
GEORGE ALLEN & UNWIN LTD
RUSKIN HOUSE   MUSEUM STREET

FIRST PUBLISHED IN 1963

This book is copyright under the Berne Convention. Apart from any fair dealing for the purpose of private study, research, criticism or review, as permitted under the Copyright Act, 1956, no portion may be reproduced by any process without written permission. Enquiries should be addressed to the publisher.

© Rupert Furneaux, 1963

PRINTED IN GREAT BRITAIN
in 11 on 12 point Juliana type
BY THE BLACKFRIARS PRESS LTD
LEICESTER

When my father was writing from the 1940s to the 1970s, his purpose was to make subjects like *Massacre at Amritsar* available to the general public in an easy to understand, straightforward style. Why? Because he was dyslexic and interested in history. Not the perfect combination when most books on such subjects were written by academics mostly for academics. I too am dyslexic, and I too am interested in history. While it is easy now to find information in a format that suits me, it was not so when he was writing.

He did extensive research for his books and this one was no exception. Rupert Furneaux recreated the scenes of the Jallianwala Bagh massacre from accounts of eyewitnesses and of survivors. He looked at the circumstances that led up to it and the actions that followed it. He looked into the mind of General Dyer for clues as to why that order was given. During the 1960s, according to a retired Army Officer of my acquaintance, this event was taught to soldiers of the British Army as "this is how it should NOT be done" with reference to crowd control.

My father was an opinionated man -- born in the Edwardian era,1908 -- but he did not follow the path expected of him. Perhaps a bit bohemian, he became a film producer, and worked for the BBC, before becoming a full-time author in 1950. He died in 1980.

Drusilla Furneaux
March 2022

CONTENTS

I.	Conception of Duty	page 13
II.	The Jallianwala Bagh	15
III.	Riot or Rebellion?	33
IV.	Flare Up in Amritsar	48
V.	General Dyer Takes Command	69
VI.	'The Decisive Factor'	79
VII.	The Crawling Order	88
VIII.	Martial Law	99
IX.	Dyer Reports	105
X.	The Soldier	112
XI.	Enquiry	119
XII.	Censure	128
XIII.	Controversy	139
XIV.	Justification	144
XV.	Decision	153
XVI.	Libel	161
XVII.	The Story Ends with Murder	168
BIBLIOGRAPHY		180
INDEX		181

ACKNOWLEDGMENTS

Grateful acknowledgment is made to the Librarian, the India Office, for the loan of printed papers, to the Librarian, Associated Newspapers Ltd., for permission to examine their files, and for permission to quote from William Blackwood & Sons Ltd. (Ian Colvin, *Life of General Dyer* and *An Englishwoman*), Hutchinson & Co. (Gen. Sir George Barrow, *Life of Sir Charles Carmichael Monro*), Constable & Co. (Sir Michael O'Dwyer, *India As I Knew It*) and Faber and Faber Ltd. (Edward Thompson, *A Letter from India*). With the exception of the frontispiece, the photographs reproduced in this book were kindly provided by the former India Office Library, now the Commonwealth Relations Office.

ILLUSTRATIONS

Brigadier-General R. E. H. Dyer   *frontispiece*

1 Jallianwala Bagh, scene of the massacre   *facing page* 32
    The Bazar leading to the Jallianwala Bagh

2 The position from which the soldiers fired   33
    One of the narrow exits from the Jallianwala Bagh

3 The Kucha Kaurianwala where Miss Sherwood
    was attacked   48
    A boy showing where Miss Sherwood took shelter

4 The National Bank at Amritsar after the rioting   49
    The room in the Alliance Bank at Amritsar where
    Mr Thompson was murdered

MAP OF AMRITSAR

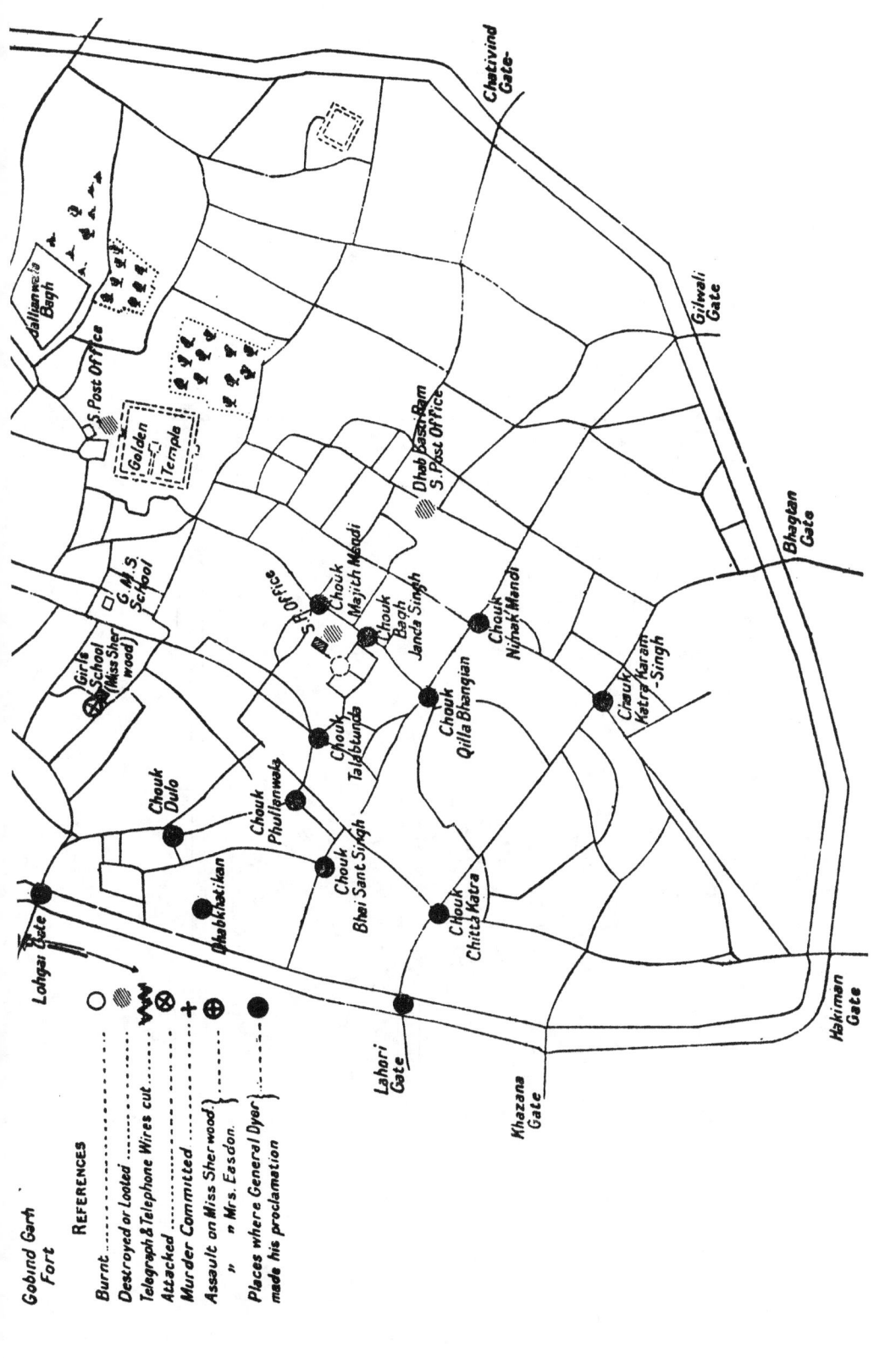

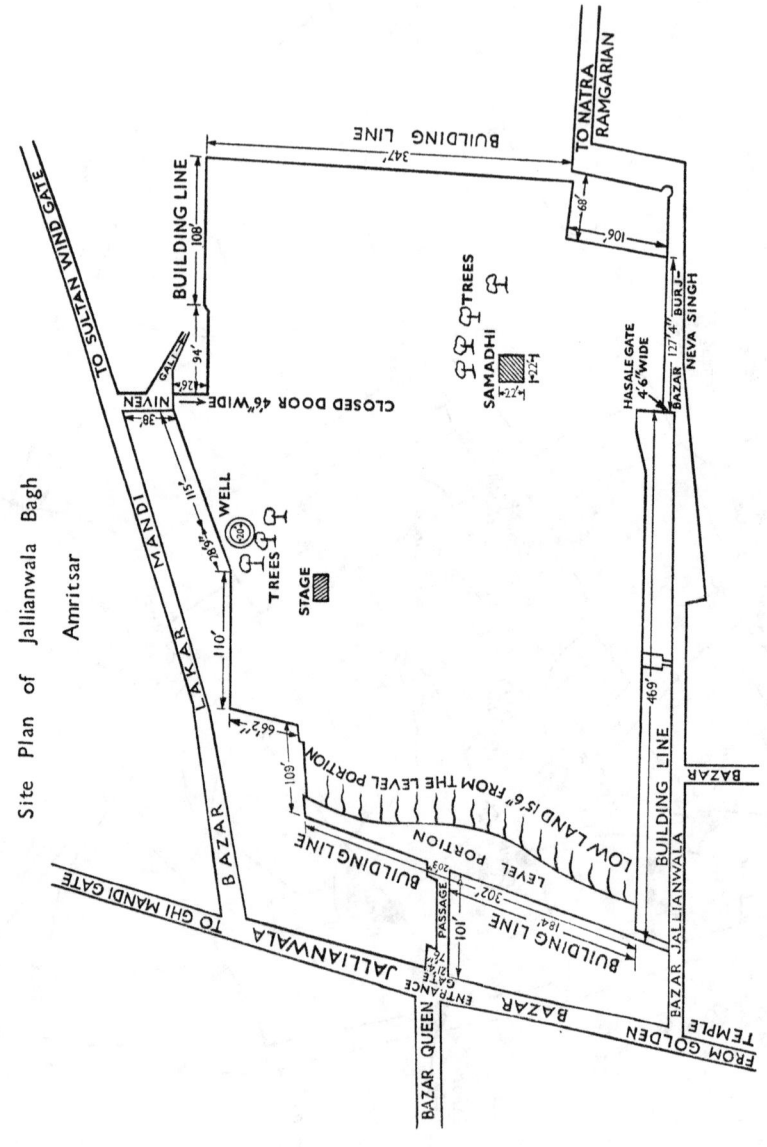

I

CONCEPTION OF DUTY

'I fired and continued to fire until the crowd dispersed, and I consider this is the least amount of firing which would produce the necessary moral and widespread effect it was my duty to produce if I was to justify my action. If more troops had been at hand the casualties would have been greater in proportion. It *was no longer a question of merely dispersing the crowd*, but one of producing a sufficient moral effect from a military point of view not only on those who were present, but more especially throughout the Punjab. There could be no question of undue severity.'

So said General Dyer on August 25, 1919, a statement to which he stuck for the rest of his life, words which branded him in the eyes of millions as an inhuman monster, a British soldier who had committed an appalling atrocity, one for which he found no adequate excuse necessary.

In 1920 the controversy about General Dyer's action in the Jallianwala Bagh at Amritsar in the Punjab on April 13, 1919, divided England into two angry claques, those who clamoured that, by shooting down 379 natives and wounding 1,200 others, Dyer had taught the 'bloody browns' a lesson, and thereby saved India from a second Mutiny, and those who protested that he had committed an unexampled act of brutality and perpetrated a deliberately calculated massacre, the blackest spot on England's escutcheon since the burning at the stake of Joan of Arc, an act of terrorism which, far from saving India, ignited the spark of Indian nationalism, an act of 'frightfulness' which resulted twenty-eight years later in Britain losing the brightest jewel in her Imperial Crown. A demonstration of Britain's might which boomeranged with a vengeance.

Brigadier General Reginald Edward Harry Dyer died in 1927. The British Raj is no more. The White Sahibs are gone from India. Outside India the Jallianwala Bagh is forgotten, its memory blotted out by more infamous deeds at Lidice, Hiroshima and Sharpeville.

In 1920 Dyer was thrown to the wolves. Whatever the iniquity or merit of his act, outraged Indian opinion needed to be placated. Political expediency demanded his punishment. In an unexampled act of faith the Tories of Britain rallied to his support. An English judge exonerated him. But the Indians did not forget; in 1940 Dyer's political superior and principal supporter fell victim to an assassin's bullet.

The 'breaking' of Dyer and the shot that killed Sir Michael O'Dwyer left many questions unanswered.

Was Dyer's 'horrible' though 'merciful' act, as he called it, entirely justified or was it sheer massacre, an appalling atrocity? Or a terrible error of judgment? Or a ghastly mistake? Why did he fire without warning and prolong the firing for ten minutes? What extraordinary psychological process led him to change his story? Why did he refuse to justify himself, in the only way which could have exculpated him? Then there is the larger query. Can a man be guilty of an atrocity while acting with complete integrity? And the lesser one. Did the Government of the day depreciate Dyer's clumsiness rather than his crime?

To seek answers to these questions we need to take ourselves to the tortuous, torrid streets of Amritsar. It is Sunday, April 13, 1919, a hot afternoon in early summer.

II

THE JALLIANWALA BAGH

The open cars carrying the officers, preceded by two policemen on horseback and followed by two armoured cars, ninety men marching in front and behind, their measured pace dictating the column's speed, clattered through the sun-baked streets. Halfway down the bazaar, at the Commanding Officer's signal, the cortege came to an abrupt halt. At the side of the bazaar opened a narrow lane, contracting within a few yards into a cramped passage, $7\frac{1}{2}$ feet wide, too restricted to allow the entry of the armoured cars equipped with machine guns.

Into the lane, at the officer's command, the soldiers marched in double file. From beyond the walls enclosing it came the buzz of a restless crowd. Above droned an aeroplane, symbol of white man's might. Debouching from the passage the soldiers deployed right and left, taking position on a narrow platform overlooking the eight acre open space stretching away to the south, an uneven piece of waste ground almost totally enclosed by the walls of the adjoining buildings, a barren rectangle filled by an enormous crowd which stood and sat listening to a speaker gesticulating on a platform, too far from the entrance for his words to be heard. At the officer's command the twenty-five armed men on either side of the entrance crouched and levelled their rifles, the forty men armed only with knives standing behind them. 'Fire', ordered the officer.

As the soldiers emerged from the passage the crowd half turned and from thousands of throats came the low murmur 'Look; see the soldiers come'. Those squatting in groups began to rise; men standing with children astride their shoulders lowered them to the ground. ('I saw a number of children sitting on the shoulders of the men' states Lala Parmanand, who was perched on the edge of a roof of a temple fifteen feet above the soldiers.) Some of the crowd began to run.

'Don't be afraid' cried the speaker on the platform, Hans Raj, 'they will not fire on innocent men. Stay where you are,' he ordered. The people hesitated. 'Remain seated', he told them, jumping down from his dais and running towards the soldiers, waving a white handkerchief. Mian Abdul Aziz, aged thirty, tried to slip away through the main gate. He was beaten back by the soldiers' rifle butts.

When the firing began, Hans Raj shouted 'They are only blanks; remain where you are'. Again the crowd hesitated. Bullets whined overhead. 'Why are you firing high?' Pratap Singh, a carpenter from a neighbouring village, heard the officer shout. 'Fire low, for what else have you been brought here?' he heard him order. A whistle sounded and the fire swept the ground. People started to run in all directions. 'All was utter confusion' was all that Soham Lal, a baker, could remember afterwards. He made a dash for a tiny passage between the walls of two houses, climbing the wall with Hans Raj and throwing himself down on the other side.

The shooting down in cold blood of some 1,500 Indians in the death-trap of the Jallianwala Bagh, a word meaning the 'garden' of one 'Jallian', more accurately an unkempt piece of waste ground, a 'dunghill' as Mahatma Gandhi called it, on the afternoon of April 13th, by General Dyer, was described five months later by a number of survivors and Indian eye-witnesses who gave evidence before the National Congress Sub-Committee of Enquiry, presided over by Gandhi, who is described by a member of that Committee, a barrister of the High Court of Bombay, M. R. Jayakar, as 'taking infinite pains to see that what was put before the public was the quintessence of truth'. The testimony given by these Indian witnesses, he says, was carefully sifted and each man was cross examined and warned of the risks they were running in giving such evidence. Testimony was given also to the official Hunter Committee of Enquiry by a British police officer present and by General Dyer himself. From the eye-witness descriptions of these people, brown and white, it is possible to recreate the scene of slaughter, one which had no modern parallel until the Nazis wiped out the Czech village of Lidice and the South African police mowed down the black crowd at Sharpeville.

The white men in their testimony were terse and colourless. Back of the smoking rifles they were spectators, safe, detached and observant only of the general scene. The brown witnesses on the roofs of neighbouring buildings or fugitives on the ground below, saw the massacre only in the tiny detail of their own personal experience, as they watched horror-struck or ran or hid to escape the flying bullets.

That morning General Dyer had marched through the city and at nineteen points at beat of drum a proclamation was read forbidding processions or meetings and warning, in General Dyer's words, that 'any such procession or any gathering of four men would be looked upon and treated as an unlawful assembly and dispersed by force of arms if necessary'.

In his dispatch, dated August 25th, in respect of the shooting, Dyer stated:

'I considered it my *bounden duty to disperse by fire* the unlawful assembly.

'The gathering in the Jallianwala Bagh must have received ample warning of my coming, and I personally had ample time to consider the nature of the painful act I might be faced with.

'I was faced by a dense mass of men evidently holding a seditious meeting.'

He did not consult anyone, Dyer said, for there was no one to consult. 'I had to make up my mind immediately what my action should be', he told the Hunter Committee. 'I considered it from a military view that I should fire immediately, that, if I did not do so, I should fail in my duty.'

'My mind was made up as I came along in my motor car', he stated. If his orders were not obeyed he would fire immediately. When he was asked if he had decided what he was going to do during the march, he declared, 'I had made up my mind. I was only wondering whether I should do it or whether I should not.'

To further questions he replied:

'The responsibility was very great. If I fired I must fire with good effect, a small amount of firing would be a criminal act of folly.

'There was no reason to further parley with the mob, evidently they were there to defy "the arm of the law".'

General Dyer gave the crowd no warning of his intentions; no hint of what was to come. At the Hunter Committee of Enquiry he was asked:

'What did you do?'
'I opened fire.'
'At once?'
'Immediately. I had thought about the matter and it did not

take me more than thirty seconds to make up my mind to where my duty was.'

No warning was given to the people to disperse, testified Girdhari Lal, a business man watching the meeting through binoculars from a nearby roof. He saw Gurkhas with rifles in their hands rush into the Bagh and take position on the raised ground which covered the canal carrying water to the Golden Temple. 'The people were all running when the firing began,' stated Lala Karan Chand, aged twenty-nine, an assistant accountant, 'the soldiers came in and formed into line at once, and there was no warning given at all. They began to fire at once.' Sardar Arjan Singh, thirty-one, a shopkeeper, watching from a roof described what he saw: 'The military opened fire without asking the people to disperse. They never gave any warning. At first the soldiers fired high, but the Sahib ordered them to fire straight and low.' His testimony was confirmed by Pratap Singh: 'The soldiers began to fire at once. No warning was given. The first volley was fired high. On this the officer reprimanded the Gurkhas with a revolver pointed at them, he abused them in filthy language.' Captain Briggs, General Dyer's Brigade-Major, states in his report, 'The men did not hesitate to fire low and I saw no man firing high.'

In obedience to the command, the soldiers lowered their rifles; their fire swept the ground. On the second volley 'the people began to fall down', stated Ram Saran Singh, aged thirty, and he explained: 'I was about to run also when a Sikh, presumably a retired military man, told me to lie flat to save myself'. Some ran, others lay down, says Pratap Singh, an employee in a perfumer's shop. 'I sat down and pulled down my son', he says. They lay at full length. The shots came whizzing past and many fell. 'All the people began to run in all directions', states Lala Hardyal Lal, aged forty-five, who told the Congress Sub-Committee, 'many fell while running away'. 'The firing was directed towards people who were running away', noticed Sardar Aryan Singh from his vantage point on the roof of a shop. 'The firing was continued on the people, especially aimed towards the entrances from where the people were going out', saw Pratap Singh, who was fortunate enough to crawl to the wall, behind the soldiers' guns.

'I merely felt that my orders had not been obeyed, that Martial Law was flouted, and that it was my duty to immediately disperse it (the assembly) by rifle fire', stated General Dyer in his dispatch. In his testimony to the Hunter Committee he said:

'I had made up my mind that I would do all men to death if they were going to continue the meeting.'

A remark that so astonished General Sir George Barrow, a member of the Committee, that it remained in his memory and he recalled it in his *Life of General Sir Charles Monro*, 1931.

Earlier Dyer had been questioned by Lord Hunter:

'In firing was your object to disperse the crowd?'
'Yes.'
'Any other object?'
'No, sir. I was going to fire until they dispersed.'
'Did the crowd at once start to disperse as soon as you fired?'
'Immediately.'
'Did you continue firing?'
'Yes.'
'If the crowd was going to disperse, why did you not stop firing?'
'I thought it my duty to go on firing until it dispersed. If I fired a little, the effect would not be sufficient. If I fired a little I should be wrong in firing at all.'
'How long did the firing go on?'
'It may be ten minutes; it may be less, calculated from the number of rounds that we fired.'

General Dyer agreed that the crowd was unarmed, even with sticks.

'What reason had you to suppose that if you had ordered the assembly to leave the Bagh, they would not have done so without the necessity of your firing, continued firing for a length of time?"
'Yes; I think it quite possible that I could have dispersed them even without firing.'
'Why did you not adopt that course?'
'I could not disperse them for some time; then they would all come back and laugh at me, and I considered I would be making myself a fool.'
'In your view the situation was a very serious one?'
'Very serious indeed, Sir.'

The terrified crowd, estimated by General Dyer at the time to number 5,000 but which was afterwards agreed to have numbered at least 25,000 people, surged outwards, splitting into two vast waves, both vainly trying to escape the torturing bullets which continued to fly for fifteen minutes, says Girdhari Lal 'without any perceptible break'. Through his field glasses, he saw 'hundreds of persons killed on the spot'. The two waves, he saw, rushed for the walls at the sides of the Bagh, seeking escape from the holocaust of lead, searching for narrow passages between the encircling houses. Many people were hit in the back, says Pandit Chet Ram, a thirty-five-year-old court pleader, caught in the maelstrom of frantic men. Others were trampled under foot, he testified. Those who exposed themselves, trying to climb the walls, were picked off by the soldiers, asserts Lala Hari Saran, a broker. 'The soldiers continued firing in the direction in which the crowd was running', stated Dr Mani Ram who peeped back through a hole in the wall he had managed to climb. 'I could not climb over the wall', said Lala Gian Chand. He dropped down and put his face between his knees. 'People fell over me', he said. Later he managed to leap over the wall, falling headlong on its further side.

Lala Ramgopal, twenty-eight-year-old son of a confectioner, managed to scramble over a pile of dead bodies and climb the wall but he lost his doti in the process and found himself running down a side street completely naked. Mian Mohammed Sharif, twenty-four, a street trader, as he ran was hit by a bullet in the thigh. In front of him was a fat man trying to climb the wall. Sharif climbed over him, jumped the wall and escaped. A Sikh gentleman, he says, living in a house bordering the Bagh, saved many by helping them climb the wall. Lala Karan Chand found the narrow passage he reached blocked by a wall as high as his chest; the fugitives could climb it only one by one. As he waited his turn, he saw those behind him being shot down. He tried to crouch down. Then he spotted what looked like a better chance of escaping the bullets. A trap door into the canal was broken, he saw. He managed to lower himself through it, one leg at a time, and he got into the water up to his waist. Three other men slipped in beside him. Others threw themselves into a well near the eastern wall of the Bagh, the earlier arrivals being drowned by the weight of the people falling on top of them. Seth Lakhrim Chand, a thirty-two-year-old piece-goods merchant, when he reached a passage in the wall, found it blocked by 150 corpses.

As he tried to climb over the obstruction he was shot in the ankle, losing consciousness. He escaped finally but his leg had to be amputated below the knee.

'When the firing commenced what was the crowd doing?' R. Plomer, Deputy Superintendent of Police, was asked by Lord Hunter. 'Rushing in the opposite direction,' he replied, adding that they were trying to escape as far as they could. Captain Briggs said that when the firing began, the crowd broke into two bodies, and he explained in his report, 'Things were getting very serious indeed, and it looked as though they were going to rush. Fire was ordered first on one lump of crowd, which looked the most menacing, and then on the other.'

In his evidence, Dyer stated that from time to time he changed the firing and directed it to places where the crowd was thickest. Came this question:

'It was unlikely that a man shooting into the crowd would miss?'

Came this answer:

'No, according to the circumstances of the case. They were running, and I noticed only a certain number of men were hit. In the centre of the section, the crowd was very dense and therefore if a man directed his fire well he should not miss.'

Unable to squeeze through the tiny exits, only four or five in number, each less than $4\frac{1}{2}$ feet wide, the waves rebounded from the walls too high to climb. Twenty-five thousand frantic people surged back towards the soldiers whose fire was so rapid that Girdhari Lal incorrectly got the impression that quick-firing guns were being used. He told the Congress Sub-Committee:

'The worst part of the whole thing was that the firing was directed towards the gates through which the people were running out. There were small outlets, four or five in all, and bullets actually rained over the people at all these gates. Shots were also fired into the thick of the meeting. There was not a corner left of the garden facing the firing line where people did not die in large numbers. Many got trampled under the feet of the rushing crowds and thus lost their lives. Blood was pouring in profusion. Even those who lay flat on the ground were shot, as I saw the Gurkhas kneel down and fire.'

Dyer thought that when the crowd surged back from the walls

of the Bagh, it was massing to charge him and his small band of men. He stated on August 25th:

'The crowd was so dense that if a determined rush had been made at any time, arms or no arms, my small force must instantly have been overpowered and consequently I was very careful of not giving the mob a change of organizing. I sometimes ceased fire and redirected my fire where the crowd was collecting more thickly.'

Hurled back from the walls, the crowds poured across the Bagh like a flock of frightened sheep. Some ran wildly about seeking shelter from the whizzing bullets. Others threw themselves to the ground. 'People were falling everywhere', noticed an elderly man named Mulchand. Ram Saran Singh, already on the ground, was submerged by wounded men. Although not hurt himself, his clothes became saturated by their blood. Lala Guranditta, flinging himself down, saw the soldiers lowering their aim to sweep the ground, and he was hit twice in the leg. Beside him he noticed a young boy of twelve lying dead with a child aged about three dead in his arms. Wazir Ali, a thirty-five-year-old teacher, was struck in the right eye. Around him, he says, were heaps of dead and dying. Lala Mansa Ram, a broker, was hit in the stomach by a bullet.

Ismail, aged twenty, the son of a butcher, watching from a neighbouring house, saw men falling everywhere. 'Hundreds of them', he testified later. Abdul Ahad, sixty, a shawl maker, saw twelve people sheltering behind a tree, standing one behind the other. The soldiers spotted them. One after another they dropped to the ground as the bullets found them. 'There were short intervals in the firing', says Dr Mani Ram, 'when those who were lying on the ground tried to get to their feet.' They were at once fired upon, he told the Congress Sub-Committee. He escaped injury and that night, searching the Bagh, he stumbled over the corpse of his son.

Lala Bodh Raj, twenty-nine, the son of the proprietor of a chemical factory, hid behind a tomb which stood in the Bagh. For some minutes he watched people falling everywhere. Then he managed to crawl the 150 yards to the wall and climb over it. A seventeen-year-old shop employee named Nathi hid himself in the trunk of a decayed tree. Pratap Singh, who was lying flat with his son, says, 'Men began to run again and I ran to the other side of the (speaker's) platform and fell flat there. There was quite a heap of bodies and I was protected from the bullets by them.'

Girdhari Lal says that he heard afterwards that Mr Rehill, the Superintendent of Police, and Inspector Jawahar Lal could not bear to see the firing and went outside the Bagh to avoid the sight. Neither of these men were able to give the Hunter Committee any detailed story of the firing.

Asked by an Indian member of the Hunter Committee if his idea was 'to strike terror?' General Dyer replied, 'Call it what you like. I was going to punish them. My idea from the military point of view was to make a wide impression.' The crowd had defied him, he said, and he declared 'I was going to give them a lesson'. He was asked particularly:

'Did you observe after the firing opened a number of people lying on the ground in order to save themselves?'

'Yes.'

'And you continued to fire on these people who were lying on the ground?'

'I cannot say that. I think that some were running at the time and I directed their fire; and sometimes I stopped firing and redirected to fire on other targets. The firing was controlled.'

'Did you direct the firing on the people who were lying down to save themselves?'

'I probably selected another target. I might have been firing on the people who were lying down though I think there were better targets than that.'

The firing lasted about ten minutes, according to General Dyer's estimate. One thousand six hundred and fifty rounds of Mark VI, ·303 rifle ammunition had been fired, he found when the soldiers' pouches were examined on their return to headquarters. He stopped the firing, he said, because ammunition was running low. He had been unable to bring in the armoured cars, equipped with machine guns, he stated. If it had been possible to bring them into the Bagh the casualties might have been heavier, he thought. When he was asked, 'Would you have opened fire with machine guns?' he answered, 'I think probably yes'.

Questioned by a member of the Hunter Committee if his action did not represent 'frightfulness', a word which for four and a half years had been used to describe the German atrocities in Belgium and France, Dyer replied:

'No, I don't think so. I think it was a horrible duty for me to perform. It was a merciful fact that I had given them a chance to disperse. The responsibility was very great. I had made up my mind that if I fired I must fire well and strong so that it would have a full effect. I had decided if I fired one round I must shoot a lot of rounds or I must not shoot at all. My logical conclusion was that I must disperse the crowd which had defied the arm of the law. I fired and continued to fire until the crowd dispersed.'

The people of Amritsar had defied his orders, Dyer declared. To disperse them was a merciful though a horrible act. His choice lay in 'carrying out a very distasteful and horrible duty or neglecting to do my duty, of suppressing disorder or of becoming responsible for all future bloodshed'. 'The necessity was very great indeed', he told the Hunter Committee appointed to investigate the 'Disorders in the Punjab'. The means justified the end. Open rebellion reigned in Amritsar and it was his duty to suppress it. Every man who escaped from the Bagh was a 'messenger', he emphasized, 'to tell that law and order had been restored in Amritsar'.

The majority of the 25,000 natives who had assembled in the Jallianwala Bagh, contrary to General Dyer's orders, lived to tell the story of their punishment for disobedience. The effect of the shooting was 'electric', Deputy Commissioner Miles Irving told the Hunter Committee. The news of the shooting as it spread ended the danger of further disturbances, he stated.

The exact number of natives killed in the Jallianwala Bagh will never be known accurately. Officially they are estimated at 379 killed, with at least 1,200 persons wounded, but Indian opinion rates both figures far higher. The firing started between 5 and 5.15 p.m. It was over in ten to fifteen minutes. Then the soldiers left. At General Dyer's command, they rose to their feet, shouldered their rifles and marched off, fifty nameless brown men who, at the orders of their white officer, shot down their kinsmen without compunction and, as far as we know, without regret. It was their duty. They had been trained to obey orders. If they had refused to fire, they might have been shot themselves.

No arrangements were made by the British authorities to succour the wounded or dispose of the dead. When he was asked at the meeting of the Hunter Committee at which he testified whether he had done anything to relieve the wounded, Dyer replied, 'No, certainly not'. It was not his job, he said.

General Dyer, when he marched his men away from the Bagh, left behind him a scene of horror. At least 1,500 Indians, subjects of his King-Emperor, lay either dead or writhing in agony from wounds great or small. Many of them were children. Over 20,000 people struggled frantically to escape from the death-trap in which they had been caught. Scrambling over piles of bodies, fighting with their neighbours for right of passage, they thrust themselves through the tiny exits or climbed the walls and ran to their homes. Two and a half hours only remained until curfew, when, if caught in the streets, they could be shot down. Those Indians who returned to the Bagh that night to seek relatives and friends or to succour the wounded risked death.

Girdhari Lal went to look for a friend. He found himself stumbling over corpses:

'There were heaps of them at different places, and people were turning over dead bodies to recognize their relations or friends. The dead bodies were of grown up people and young boys also. At or near the gates the number was very large, and bodies were scattered in large numbers all over the garden. Some had their heads cut open, others had eyes shot, and nose, chest, arms or legs shattered. It was a fearful and ghastly sight. I think there must have been over one thousand dead bodies in the garden then . . .

'I saw people were hurrying up, and many had to leave their dead and wounded, because they were afraid of being fired upon again after 8 p.m. Many amongst the wounded, who managed to run away from the garden, succumbed on their way to the injuries received, and lay dead in the streets. It was thus that the people of Amritsar held their Baisakhi fair.'

Girdhari Lal was referring to the annual horse and cattle fair held in Amritsar on April 13th to which the villagers from the surrounding country came each year, many of them men who could not possibly have heard General Dyer's warning proclamation that morning.

When the firing finished Pratap Singh found himself unharmed. He told the Congress Sub-Committee:

'I got up and saw bodies on all sides, and went towards the back of the garden. The bodies were so thick about the passage, that I could not find my way out. I had my son with me and men were rushing over the dead bodies. I took my son also over the dead bodies. In my opinion there must have been nearly 2,000 dead bodies in the garden. Nearly all my clothes were left behind. I never saw any lathis (sticks) the whole time I was there, neither among those sitting nor on the ground afterwards. The pagri (turban) and shoes of my son were also lost. As I was creeping near the dead bodies, I slipped and fell and lost hold of my son. The people behind, now began trampling over me, and I had many blows and wounds on my chest. All my breath was taken out of me and I thought I was dying. When the rush was over, I revived and got out from amongst the dead bodies and ran into the lane. I had no dhotie, only a shirt and a coat I had. I could not speak. I was stunned and went into some house. I don't know whose it was. Just then I heard someone saying, 'They are coming again; they are coming again'. I rushed out and fled down another lane. On the road I was so thirsty that I could not run or stand any more. I took some water from an old woman at the well and asked for a loin cloth. Then I began crying, 'Has anyone seen my child?' but no one had seen him. I ran home and found my son had not reached there. My relations went in all directions to find him. After half an hour the boy came back himself. After that for some twenty to twenty-five days I was very ill in bed, and could not sit up.'

Another survivor, Lala Gian Chand, stated:

'After the firing was over, I saw about five or six hundred persons of all ages, including the dead and the wounded, lying about in the street, outside the Bagh. I reached my house with the greatest difficulty, and there I learnt that my two nephews were not in the house. I then went back to look for them in the garden. I found heaps of dead bodies and wounded men near the exits. On reaching the garden, I found my nephew's body riddled with bullets. His skull was broken. There was one shot under his nose on the upper lips, two on the left side, one on the left neck, and three on the thigh and some two or three on the head.'

The story told by Mian Sikander Ali was as follows:

'I immediately left for the Bagh to search for my younger son. I reached the Bagh at about 7.15 p.m. entering in through the main entrance on the north. I managed to extricate his dead body from a large heap of corpses near the outlet to the east of the well. The deceased had a bullet mark on his calf, and a big opening a little over his forehead. Close to my son, lay my cousin, named Ismail. He also had received a bullet on his calf, and his right jaw had been lacerated. A near relation of Ismail, named Hasan, had also come to the Bagh in search of the latter. We both removed the two corpses with the greatest difficulty, as there was no one to help us. There were a number of children among the dead. I saw an aged man lying prostrate on the ground with a two years old baby in his arms. Both appeared to be lifeless. The number of the dead and wounded, then lying in the garden, was about two thousand.'

Lala Karan Chand, we recall, escaped death by hiding himself in the canal. When the firing ceased, he was surprised by a Sikh who came to get water for the wounded. He enquired if the soldiers had gone and upon being reassured he asked the man to 'catch hold of me and get me out'. He was pulled out and he ran into the street, where he changed his wet clothes in a shop. His story continues:

'Then I came back into the Bagh, because I thought the wounded ought to be taken to the doctor. I went in at the entrance opposite the Samadh. I saw a very tall Sikh who was wounded in the leg, and who had made a splint of a small stick. Some man brought a charpai (cot) and carried him off and I left him. There were many people wounded; and I found a Marwari wounded in the leg. We carried him through the Main Gate (that through which the soldiers came) and put him down in the Queen's Bazaar. Then, as I was going back again, I met my father and my brother; and they told me that my elder brother was missing. Then we went to seek for him by way of Bazaar Jallianwala. I met many wounded men and children; and there were the dead also in Bazaar Burj Mewa Singh. Then we went into the garden again. There were heaps of the dead piled one upon another, and people were carrying them away. We searched and searched, and at the wall facing the main entrance, we found his body. He was on the further side of the wall. His legs were covered with bricks, and a shot had gone through his mouth. My brother and I took him up and found a charpai when we got back as far as Bazaar Mewa Singh, and we took him home. While I was searching for my brother, I saw the Bagh was like a battlefield. There were corpses scattered everywhere in heaps, and the wounded were crying out for water. I saw many bodies of children. I saw one boy of about twelve years old being carried out, just at the time we were carrying out the dead. I looked into the passage from which I escaped, and there were the dead in heaps. My friend, Wasumall, was wounded in the side and died about four days after. By far, the greater number of the corpses was along the back wall and in the corners. I never saw any lathis at all in the Bagh when I was searching for my brother.'

Sardar Partap Singh, a bookseller, told the Congress Sub-Committee:

'I did not go to Jallianwala Bagh at the time of the meeting on April 13th. My son, Sundar Singh, had gone to attend that meeting. When I heard the firing in the Jallianwala Bagh, I ran towards the Bagh to find out my son. I saw many people wounded lying on the way. When I reached there, I saw the soldiers returning from the Jallianwala Bagh. They were at a distance of about 100 yards from me. The soldiers were about forty in number. I did not enter the Jallianwala Bagh from the side from which the soldiers had come out, because I was afraid, but went round and entered by jumping over a wall. Dead bodies were lying on all sides near the enclosure walls. When I entered, a dying man asked for water. There is a drain which carries water from the canal to Darbar Sahab. It is called Hansli. The drain is covered, but there is a pit connected with it which is about four feet square. When I tried to take water from that pit, I saw many dead bodies floating in it. Some living men had also hid themselves in it, and they asked me, 'Are they (i.e. soldiers) gone?' When I told them that they had gone, they came out of it and ran away. Then I went into the middle of the Bagh to find out my son. There were about 800 or 1,000 wounded and dead lying near the walls of the Bagh, besides others who ran away wounded and died either in their own houses or in the surrounding lanes. I remained there from fifteen to twenty minutes, but could not find my son. I heard the wailing of those shot and who were crying for water. Then I ran back home and heard that my son was safe. I asked three or four men to accompany me to the Jallianwala Bagh and give water to the dying and wounded. We took vessels and came back to Jallianwala Bagh and gave water to some of the wounded. I did not hear any proclamation on the 13th, forbidding people to attend public meetings; nor did I hear that any such proclamation had been made in the bazaar.'

Ram Saran Singh, thirty years of age, one of those who

escaped from the Bagh, learned when he reached home that his sister's husband had not returned. After he had changed his clothes, he went back to the garden. His story goes on:

'I saw about 1,000 persons lying scattered all over the garden. There were a large number of these near the entrance to the Bagh, including many young boys. There were dead bodies in the adjacent lanes also. I turned over many dead bodies, but could not trace my brother-in-law. I returned home. Late in the evening, my sister told me that her husband had not come home. Early in the morning on 14th, I again went to the garden with three or four other persons. I saw people removing dead bodies even then. I found my relative's dead body in the canal amongst the other corpses. He had three bullets. One on the forehead and another on the side, and the third in the back. I brought my relative's body to his house in the Nimak Mandi, and removed it from there to the cremation grounds at Chattiwind Gate. The place was full of dead bodies burning, and we had to cremate my relation out in the open; and there were many others being cremated likewise. There was no one to record the number of deaths.'

Many other stories were told of the aftermath of the Jallianwala Bagh blood bath. Khushal Singh, an auctioneer, found many small children amongst the victims, whom he estimated at 2,000 killed and wounded. Amin Chand, vendor of aerated waters, found piles of bodies along the boundary walls and the dead and dying covered the ground. Mir Riaz-ul-Hasan, aged nineteen, came across heaps of corpses at the two small exits along the south-eastern wall. Other heaps lay in the corners of the Bagh and by the canal. The corpses were ten to twelve feet high in places, says Mohammed Ismail, aged twenty. The heaps near the well and near the speaker's platform were particularly large. He thought, he told the Congress Sub-Committee, that there had been four or five hundred children present. Pandit Chet Ram, court pleader, estimated the dead at 500. Most of the bodies he saw had been hit in the back. Many had died, he says, from being trampled underfoot in the mad stampede. Mian Husain Shah, aged thirty-five, who had watched the shooting from the privy of his house, states that there were big heaps of bodies at the outlets. Lala Nathir Ram, a thirty-five-year-old contractor, searching for his son and brother, turned over heaps of corpses. He found the body of his brother under three or four others near the foot of the raised ground from where the soldiers had marched away five minutes before. He turned over two hundred bodies at that spot alone, he says. He estimated the dead at 1,500 and, he says, the kites were already hovering low in expectation of a feast. They were so voracious, he found, that 'it was with the greatest difficulty one could keep one's turban on one's head'. Sardar Arjan Singh, the shopkeeper who had a grandstand view of the shooting, went into the Bagh after the soldiers left, finding 1,500 to 1,600 dead and wounded. Many, he says, were villagers who had come into the city to attend the Baisakhi Fair. The dead were piled near the exits in three or four layers, he noticed. Lala Atmaran, a broker who lived near the Bagh, heard all through the night the wounded moaning and crying out and he saw people with lanterns moving about. Lala Hardyal Mal, whose house was situated next to the main entrance to the Bagh, sat at his window on the first floor, smoking and watching the people carry the corpses.

The widow Ratan-Devi was one of those who spent the night in the Jallianwala Bagh. Let her tell her story:

'I was in my house near Jallianwala Bagh when I heard shots fired. I was then lying down. I got up at once as I was anxious, because my husband had gone to the Bagh. I began to cry, and went to the place accompanied by two women to help me. There I saw heaps of dead bodies and I began to search for my husband. After passing through that heap, I found the dead body of my husband. The way towards it was full of blood and of dead bodies. After a short time, both the sons of Lala Sundar came there; and I asked them to bring a charpai (cot) to carry the dead body of my husband home. The boys accordingly went home and I sent away the two women also. By this time, it was eight o'clock and no one could stir out of his house, because of the curfew order. I stood waiting and crying. At about 8.30 a Sikh gentleman came. There were others who were looking for someone amongst the dead. I did not know them. I entreated the Sikh gentleman to help me in removing my husband's body to a dry place, for that place was overflowing with blood. He caught the body by the head and I by the legs, and we carried it to a dry place and laid it down on a wooden block. I waited up to 10 p.m. but no one arrived there. I got up and started towards Ablowa Katra. I thought of asking some student from the Thakurdwara to help me in carrying my husband home. I had not gone far, when some man sitting in a window in an adjacent house asked me where I was going at that late hour. I said, I wanted some men to carry my husband's dead body home. He said, he was attending a wounded man and as it was past 8 p.m. nobody could help me then. Then I started towards Katra and another man asked me the same question. I made the same appeal to him and he gave me the same answer. I had gone hardly three or four steps, when I saw an old man smoking and some people sleeping by his side. I repeated the whole of my sad story to him with hands folded. He took great pity upon me and asked those men to go with me. They said that it was ten o'clock, and that they would not like to be shot down. That was no time to stir out; how could they go out so far? So I went back and seated myself by the side of my dead husband. Accidentally, I found a bamboo stick which I kept in my hand, to keep off dogs. I saw three men writhing in agony, a buffalo struggling in great pain; and a boy, about twelve years old, in agony entreated me not to leave the place. I told him that I could not go anywhere leaving the dead body of my husband. I asked him if he wanted any wrap, and if he was feeling cold, I could spread it over him. But he asked for water, but water could not be procured at that place.

'I heard the clock striking at regular intervals of one hour. At two o'clock, a Jat, belonging to Sultan village, who was lying entangled in a wall, asked me to go near him and to raise his leg. I got up and, taking hold of his clothes, drenched in blood, raised his leg up. After that, no one else came till half past five. At about six, L. Sundar Dass, his sons and some people from my street came with a charpai, and I brought my husband home. I saw other people at the Bagh in search of their relatives. I passed my whole night there. It is impossible for me to describe what I felt. Heaps of dead bodies lay there, some on their backs and some with their faces upturned. A number of them were poor innocent children. I shall never forget the sight. I was all alone the whole night in that solitary jungle. Nothing but the barking of dogs, or the braying of donkeys was audible. Amidst hundreds of corpses, I passed my night, crying and watching. I cannot say more. What I experienced that night is known only to me and to God.'

On his return to his headquarters in the Ram Bagh, outside the city, General Dyer spoke to the Deputy District Commissioner, Mr Miles Irving, who had not accompanied him. What he is then alleged to have said will be mentioned later. Neither he, nor Mr Irving, referred to these words in their evidence to the Hunter Committee and they might have remained unknown but for the curiosity of the reporter of the *Manchester Guardian*.

In order to discover the events which led General Dyer to decide to shoot down the crowd assembled in the Jallianwala Bagh, the dunghill which his act turned into an Indian national shrine, we need now to step backwards in time.

1 Jallianwala Bagh, scene of the massacre

Bazar leading to the Jallianwala Bagh

2
Left: The position from which the soldiers fired during the Jallianwala Bagh massacre

Right: One of the narrow exits from the Jallianwala Bagh

III

RIOT OR REBELLION?

General Dyer marched his men from the Jallianwala Bagh thinking, he would have us believe, that by his action in dispersing the assembly that had gathered in defiance of his orders, he had saved the Punjab from bloody revolt and all India from a second Mutiny. On his behalf it is claimed that his drastic act ended the well planned and centrally organized disturbances as suddenly as they had begun. It was a correct and merciful act, therefore, because it saved many more lives, both British and Indian, than had been taken in the Jallianwala Bagh. Dyer had a terrible duty to perform, a horrible duty which he carried out without flinching. Those, on the other hand, who declare that his shooting down of 1,500 unarmed people was atrocious and unnecessary, say that the disturbances which swept the Punjab in April 1919, and erupted simultaneously elsewhere in India, were spontaneous and unorganized, and they were already dying out when Dyer gave his ill-judged order to fire. Both camps agree that the widespread riots flared up suddenly, the spark being ignited in Delhi, the capital of India, on March 30th.

India had nobly supported the Empire in its war against Germany. Its teeming millions had contributed to the war effort both money and men and for the common cause they had endured the hardships of food scarcity, rising prices, increased taxation, the restriction of press freedom and the curtailment of personal liberty without complaint. They had been stricken by severe famine on the failure of the Monsoon in 1918 and had suffered terrible mortality from the world-wide influenza epidemic of that year. The Armistice found them restless and excited, stirred by the new spirit of personal freedom and national liberty brought to the surface throughout the world by the war, intoxicated by the new conception of the self-determination of peoples voiced by President Wilson of the United States, and agitated by the Bolshevik Revolution of 1917 which they saw as the triumph of the oppressed. The peoples of India, goaded by the ferment of the time, thought that a new dawn was breaking. Reforms had been promised by the Imperial Government, their goal Home Rule by successive stages. Great expectations had been raised. The people of India felt they had helped to win the war; now was the time for their reward. They had proved their right to be treated as an equal member of the Empire.

But, with the coming of victory, the evils from which India suffered, instead of vanishing, appeared to become aggravated. In Indian eyes the promised reforms became tarnished by modifications of an illiberal character and the wartime restrictions, embodied in the Defence of India Act of 1915, instead of being swept away, were continued in the Rowlatt Acts, the 'Black Cobras' as the peoples of India named them from a cartoon which appeared in the *Wagt* of Amritsar which depicted the Secretary of State, Mr Montagu, in the act of handing the Order of Liberty to India when a black cobra, released from a basket by Mr Rowlatt, bites her. The Rowlatt Acts were a 'pistol levelled at our breast', claimed the Indian newspaper *Vijanya*, and Mr Nehru says they were greeted with 'a wave of anger'.

The White Sahibs, who had governed India since the days of the Mutiny when the rule of the East India Company had been ended, failed to understand the strength of Indian hopes of self-government or to perceive the depth of Indian detestation of the 'Rowlatt' Acts, as they became known from the name of Sir Sydney Rowlatt, the High Court Judge who had headed the Committee appointed to investigate and propose methods of dealing with sedition. They were officially designated as the Indian Criminal Law (Amendment) Bill and the Criminal Law (Emergency Powers) Bill. According to Mr M. R. Jayakar, who became a member of the Congress Sub-Committee appointed to collect evidence on the Punjab disturbances, these Acts 'set aside all requirements of fairness and justice'. They placed infinite power in the hands of the police and of the executives so that 'even an energetic criticism of a Government measure, a religious riot, a Hindu-Muslim quarrel, might all come to be recognized as having connection with a revolutionary movement'. They gave no right of appeal and an accused person was not allowed the services of a pleader. Furthermore, he states in *The Story of My Life*, 'The authority charged with the responsibility of enforcing the Act was not to disclose to the person concerned any fact, the communication of which might engender public safety or the safety of any individual. He was compelled to submit to a trial without the protection of a single one of the safeguards which civilized countries adopt for his protection, and in making the enquiry, the authority, acting under the Act, was not bound by any of the provisions of the law of evidence.'

The Acts, he says, aroused a storm of opposition 'unknown before in India', and, according to the Congress Sub-Committee, these Acts were 'an outrage upon Society'. By the Indian masses they were labelled: 'No Appeal, No Argument, No Pleader'. Feeling against these new laws was 'widespread', admitted the Majority members of the Hunter Committee of Enquiry.

The Government of India made no attempt, beyond publishing them, to explain these Bills to the people. According to Sir Michael O'Dwyer, the Lieutenant Governor of the Punjab, they were 'a reasonable and practical measure', less drastic than the Defence of India Act, intended only to deal with revolutionary and anarchial crimes, and they were looked upon, he says, as fatal to their designs by the extremists who launched a campaign of unscrupulous misrepresentation against them.

The significance of the hated Rowlatt Acts lies, not in the true nature of their provisions, but in their effect on Indian opinion. They plunged India into the worst disturbances that had occurred since the Sepoy Mutiny of 1857 and led to riots which so terrified the whites that many believed that they faced a second Mutiny.

The passing into law of the Rowlatt Acts on March 23rd brought into being Gandhi's Passive Resistance Movement, called by him 'Satagraha', a word meaning insistence on truth, intended to replace methods of violence by a weapon which could bring the White Sahibs to their knees. A weapon soon to be sharpened by General Dyer's action at Amritsar. On February 24th Gandhi launched his campaign against the hated Acts by devising a vow in the following terms:

'Being conscientiously of opinion that the Bills . . . are unjust, subversive of the principles of liberty and justice, and destructive of the elementary rights of individuals on which the safety of the community, as a whole and the State itself is based, we solemnly affirm that in the event of these Bills becoming law and until they are withdrawn, we shall refuse civilly to obey these laws and such other laws as a committee to be hereafter appointed, may think fit, and we further affirm that in this struggle we will faithfully follow truth and refrain from violence to life, person or property.'

On March 1st a meeting of the signatories to the Satagraha

pledge was held in Bombay under the presidency of Gandhi to form a Sabha (Society) and on the following day he issued his manifesto inaugurating civil disobedience. On March 7th Gandhi attended a meeting in Delhi to protest against the Bills and similar meetings were held in other cities. A *hartal*, a day of abstinence from work and of mourning, marked by the closing of shops, was appointed by Gandhi to be held throughout India on April 6th but, through a misunderstanding, it was observed in many places on March 30th.

The *hartal* was observed in Delhi on that day by both Hindus and Muslims, all traders shutting their shops, those who refused being intimidated, the inevitable outcome of civil disobedience, which led to the first clash with the authorities. Early in the afternoon a crowd collecting at the railway station objected to the vendors selling food to passengers and they endeavoured to persuade one contractor, an old deaf man, to join the *hartal* and, when his objection that he was under contract to keep his store open failed to satisfy them, he was seized and dragged into the entrance. The Deputy Station Superintendent, who tried to help the contractor, had his coat torn off. The railway police interfered, arresting two men temporarily.

The arrest of these men evoked great excitement, and a crowd of people invaded the main station, streaming across the platforms, stopping the movement of trains, and uttering threats of violence. Mr Yule, the District Traffic Superintendent, was amongst those threatened. The crowd was driven out of the station, but it remained in the main entrance, refusing to accept the assurances given them by officials that the arrested men had been released. Members of the crowd were taken over the station buildings to satisfy themselves that no one was in custody but this failed to mollify the people who continued to demonstrate outside, stopping all traffic at the station.

About one o'clock an additional District Magistrate, Mr Gurrie, and Mr Jeffereys, an additional Superintendent of Police, arrived, the latter bringing with him a force of between forty and fifty policemen. Shortly after one o'clock, a picket of thirty soldiers and a sergeant, under the command of Lieutenant Shelford, who had been ordered to the station by Brigadier General D. H. Drake Brockman, the officer commanding the troops in Delhi, arrived on the scene. They were armed with rifles and bayonets and each man had been issued with twenty rounds of ammunition. They were joined by a party of fifteen

British soldiers who were passing through Delhi, and whose train had been held up. Lieutenant Shelford divided his men into two equal parties, commanded by Sergeant Kensley and himself.

The crowd was increasing both in numbers and in its hostility to the authorities, the station yard was packed, members of the crowd poking at Mr Jefferey's horse as he tried to push his way through. He was forced back into Queen's Road, the crowd following, finding themselves blocked by a line of police. Mr Gurrie vainly tried to persuade the crowd to break up, but they refused to disperse and kept clamouring for the release of the supposedly detained men, disbelieving the District Magistrate's protestations that they had been released. This was the situation when the Senior Superintendent of Police, Mr Marshall, arrived with a force of ten mounted policemen. Together, the line of police and soldiers slowly pressed the crowd back, bricks and stones being thrown at them. The situation became serious, the crowd completely out of hand, its hostility increasing and the throwing of stones becoming redoubled. Mr Marshall called out to Mr Gurrie they would have to fire, and at his command Sergeant Kensley's party of fifteen soldiers opened fire, killing or wounding two or three of the crowd.

This action had the desired effect, the crowd retreating towards the Town Hall and the Chadni Chowk, the main bazaar, where they were followed by the police and soldiers, who joined the line of seventeen armed constables already drawn up in front of the Town Hall. Though requested to do so, the crowd refused to disperse and they again pelted the police and soldiers with stones and proceeded to try and outflank the police line, upon which Mr Jeffereys ordered the four policemen on the extreme right to fire one round each. One man was killed but the crowd continued its advance throwing bricks, whereupon Mr Jeffereys ordered his constables to fire a volley. This had no effect and the crowd approached nearer. The firing of two volleys into the air by Sergeant Kensley's men served only to irritate the crowd and they charged the soldiers who, lowering their rifles, fired again, an action which caused the people to disperse. The casualties suffered on this occasion brought the number killed during the day to eight, many more being wounded, firing which the Hunter Committee found to have been justified in order to restore order and to prevent a disastrous outbreak of violence.

That the firing had a salutary effect was shown in the afternoon when a large meeting in the Peoples Park passed off without disturbance, but during the day a number of Europeans were molested and forced to alight from their vehicles, a fate which nearly befell General Dyer, who was in Delhi with his wife on ten days' leave. They were on a sight-seeing tour, Dyer sitting next to the chauffeur, when they came upon a multitude of people, shouting and yelling. He had just called to the ladies in the back that it must be a festival when 'two ruffians', in the words of his biographer, scrambled on to the back of the car and pulled themselves up within a few inches of the ladies. A mounted policeman dashed up and, seizing them, flung them into the road. Dyer, who did not see the incident, ordered the chauffeur to put on speed. On returning to the city later, he learnt that there had been trouble. On his return to his base at Jullundur next day, his car was hit by a stone as it passed through one village and in another a piece of wood was thrown under its wheels, clearly with the intention of upsetting it. 'During my tour I was thoroughly impressed with the dangerous nature of the feelings of the inhabitants', Dyer told the Hunter Committee.

March 30th passed off peacefully elsewhere, other towns recognizing the *hartal* on April 6th. In Gandhi's home town, Ahmedabad, a city of 400,000 people, there was no trouble and the day in Amritsar passed quietly, although all shops were shut. But the story was quite different in Lahore, the capital of the Punjab, the seat of the energetic Governor, Sir Michael O'Dwyer, who was due to retire in a few weeks after seven years of duty. Realizing from the events in Delhi that there was a storm coming, he took steps to prevent it, O'Dwyer tells us. The convening of meetings or processions in public places was banned, and he personally warned the signatories to the Satagraha Vow of the consequences of disorder if they proceeded with the proposed *hartal*. Posters were displayed, says O'Dwyer in his Memoirs, in both Amritsar and Lahore exhorting people to 'kill and die' and calling for a great rebellion on April 6th, 'our national day'.

The *hartal* in Lahore on April 6th was complete, all shops and businesses being closed, many traders being forced by open intimidation, according to O'Dwyer. The order prohibiting public meetings was openly defied, menacing crowds carrying black flags parading the streets. The Hunter Committee found that these people did not appear to be bent on violence, but

O'Dwyer says that they were prevented from forcing their way into the European Quarter only because of the presence of troops armed with machine guns. The police, who were accompanied by magistrates, induced the crowds to go back; there were no collisions but appeals to disperse were answered by cries of 'King George is dead' and Europeans were hooted and hissed. The Provincial Government attempted to counteract propaganda against the Rowlatt Acts by printing and distributing an explanation of their provisions, but this was brought to naught by the crowds tearing up the leaflets and burning them publicly. The agitators could 'thrive only on falsehood', O'Dwyer observes, and he took the opportunity to emphatically warn the opposition leaders of the dangers of their unscrupulous campaign of lies which they were carrying out amongst the ignorant masses.

Business in Lahore was resumed next day and April 6th, 7th, 8th and 9th passed off peacefully throughout the Punjab. The explosion came on the 10th. Gandhi, Sir Michael O'Dwyer learned, was on his way by train to Delhi and the Punjab. He at once passed an order forbidding his entry into the Punjab and the Government of India imposed a similar order in respect to India's capital. The exclusion of Gandhi from the danger spots was claimed by Indians afterwards to have been a direct provocation to further trouble and ill-judged, inasmuch as his presence would have lessened the disturbances and prevented violence. His journeys put the authorities in a quandary for, as he had announced that part of his programme consisted in breaking the law, if he tried to break the law they would have no option but to arrest him, which would in all probability lead to rioting and violence. However opposed Gandhi might be himself to the use of force in the prosecution of his policy, in the words of the Hunter Committee Majority Report 'there was no reason for supposing that the uneducated people of the Punjab would be equally prepared to refrain from violent methods'.

Gandhi left Bombay for Delhi on April 8th, and on learning of his progress, the Government of India directed that he should be turned back by all peaceful means and should be treated with every possible consideration and force should be used only if he refused to obey the order. Gandhi was intercepted at the railway station at Palwal, and, after protesting against the order, he agreed to return to Bombay by the next train.

When the news that Gandhi had been turned back became known, trouble flared in his home town of Ahmedabad, and in many places in the Punjab. In Delhi the shops closed but there was no actual disturbance. Serious riots occurred at Ahmedabad and in Lahore and, as we shall see, in Amritsar where their cause was local.

In Ahmedabad, the news of Gandhi's 'arrest', as rumour stated, spread rapidly on the morning of the 10th. The mill-hands ceased work and the streets were quickly filled with disorderly crowds, crying for Gandhi and enforcing the shutting of shops, and they compelled persons riding in conveyances to alight and walk as a sign of mourning. Two Europeans, named Sagar and Steeples, were forced to leave their car, whereupon they got on to a milk lorry from which they were again made to alight, and, it is suggested, incurred the anger of the crowd by making 'an impatient expression' regarding Mr Gandhi. Stones were thrown and they took refuge, first in a police post and then in a mill, which was attacked by the mob who wrecked a portion of it, demanding their surrender. Police constables from the post fired over the heads of the crowd without success and upon the owners of the mill, fearing further damage, ejecting Sagar and Steeples and the four policemen who had joined them, the party was at once set upon by the mob, the police firing in self protection, wounding twelve. One European escaped to a private bungalow and the other, who was accompanied by the four policeman, ran, pursued by the shouting crowd, climbing to the balcony of a house overlooking the street. There they were stoned by the mob, some of whom proceeded to rush the house while others lighted fires with the object of burning out the fugitives. Realizing their danger, they burrowed through the wall at the back, all but one escaping before the rioters reached the balcony. The remaining member of the party, a policeman, was assaulted and thrown to the ground below, suffering injuries from which he died next day.

When the news of the predicament of Sagar and Steeples reached Mr Chatfield, the District Commissioner, he arranged with the Superintendent of Police for the dispatch of twenty-four armed police to their rescue, both he and the Superintendent following them to the scene of the disturbance. On reaching it they saw at once that the situation was serious; the local police were absorbed in the crowd and on the ground lay the injured constable. The police car was sent to Colonel Fraser, the officer commanding troops, with a message requesting help. Mr Chatfield and the Superintendent of Police advanced on foot, joining the twenty-four constables, who had seized five members of the threatening crowd which surrounded them. For an hour and a half, the crowd pressed on the police, demanding the release of the five prisoners, which was acceded to in exchange for the dying constable, who was removed to hospital. The situation became critical, the small party of police being continually pressed back by the dangerously excited crowd, but it was relieved by the arrival of 200 soldiers who cleared the street without resort to firing. No further trouble occurred that day and in the evening a large meeting held outside the city passed off quietly.

Disturbances of great violence broke out on the 11th and there was complete defiance of authority, large crowds of millhands collecting at the Prem Gate, jeering at the military guard. Elsewhere, at the Beehive Mill, some success in dispersing a crowd was achieved by a Satagrahi who, at the request of the District Magistrate, used his influence. Nevertheless, the Magistrate and the Superintendent of Police were stoned as they drove through the city, encountering a large crowd armed with lathis, heavy iron shod sticks, which emerged from a narrow lane, mad with excitement and entirely out of the control of its leaders. A request for additional troops was sent to the cantonment and 300 Indian soldiers, under the command of Major Kirkwood, were sent with orders to fire if the mob approached within twenty-five yards or in cases of incendiarism. They were followed by 200 more soldiers commanded by Colonel Preston.

The mob committed a number of acts of incendiarism and violence before the troops arrived. One crowd set fire to a house and other crowds proceeded to burn all the government buildings, despite being fired on from a neighbouring police post. A mob which advanced on the Bank of Bombay were driven off by the police guard, who fired upon it. The gate of the jail was forced and one prisoner was released. The mobs burnt the Court House, Telegraph Office, Post Office and two police posts, and a mob surrounded the house of the civil surgeon whose wife, Mrs Tuke, brandishing a revolver, drove them off. Another mob attacked the Electric Power Station, stopping its working and severely injuring the officer in charge, Mr Brown, who was saved only by the fidelity of a workman who put the mob on a false scent. Rioters tried to seize a cart carrying ammunition, but its police guard fired and drove them off. The same mob, seeing him by himself, attempted to kill Lieutenant MacDonald, who took refuge in a building which they attacked. While a loyal Indian bicycled to the camp to bring soldiers to his rescue, MacDonald, armed with a cudgel, held a narrow stair for an hour, being continually pelted with missiles. Seeing no chance of dislodging him, the crowd set fire to the building, at which serious juncture they were driven off by troops.

By the time the troops arrived at 11 a.m., most of the government buildings had been destroyed, the fire brigade being able to save only a portion of the Telegraph Office. The area was cleared and guards posted, the crowds retreating, abusing the soldiers, throwing stones and disappearing down narrow lanes. One party of soldiers, under Lieutenant Larkin, was forced to fire when they were attacked by men armed with swords, Larkin being wounded in the arm. By noon the main streets had been cleared but outrages were committed in other parts of the city. Sergeant Fraser was dragged from a shop and murdered, his body being left in the street, the walls of the houses nearby being defaced by inscriptions which stated 'The British Raj is Gone', 'The King of England is defeated and Swaraj (Home Rule) is established', and 'Kill all Europeans; murder them wherever they be found'.

The disorders in Ahmedabad and district continued for several days. A train bringing troops from Bombay was derailed; soldiers were forced to fire again. On the 12th, when Gandhi reached the city, his commands to cease violence had a beneficial effect. In all two men had been murdered in the city and an Indian magistrate killed in the village of Viramgan nearby. Twenty-eight rioters were killed and 123 wounded. One hundred and thirty-nine charges of buckshot had been fired by the police and 609 rounds of ammunition by the troops, firing which was approved by the Hunter Committee, who found that the troops had behaved with praiseworthy restraint in most trying circumstances and that the military action was not excessive.

The news that Gandhi had been forbidden entry into the Punjab reached Lahore on the 10th and the charged atmosphere was made worse at 3.30 p.m. by the arrival of news of the outbreak at Amritsar, which will be described in the next chapter. Realizing that the turning back of Gandhi might lead to trouble, Sir Michael O'Dwyer took precautions to meet an emergency which he was convinced was well organized and prepared. The extremists were clearly determined on a trial of strength, he believed, for their inner circle knew, he states, that troops in the

Punjab were few, consisting mainly of garrisons of territorials. Attempts had been made, he declares, to tamper with these soldiers' loyalty, and he says he knew of eighteen attempts to corrupt them. Several seditious and inflammatory posters, states the Hunter Report, were put up in the city. One stated 'The English are the worst lot and are like monkeys whose deceit and cunning are obvious to all. O brethren, gird up your loins and fight, kill and be killed. Do not lose courage and try your utmost to turn out those mean monkeys from your holy country.' Another stated that the Sikh regiments in Amritsar had revolted and it urged the people of Lahore, Hindu, Muslims and Sikh, to enlist in the 'Bludgeon Army' and fight with bravery against the English monkeys. God, they were told, would grant them victory. These posters, according to the Punjab Criminal Investigation Department, were widely read and they inflamed the minds of the ignorant.

By noon military pickets had been placed at the Telegraph Office and at the Gymkhana Club, where there were a large number of white women, and at the hotels, and at 2 p.m. an urgent message was sent to General Sir William Beynon, Divisional Commander, for more troops to prevent crowds from gathering but, it being Thursday, a soldier's holiday, there was some delay in collecting and dispatching them. When he was told that military aid could not be forthcoming immediately, Sir Michael O'Dwyer went through some hours of terrible suspense, he tells us, as he expected trouble at any moment. He was holding a conference at Government House at 6 p.m. when he was informed that crowds were beginning to assemble and were attempting to march on the Civil Lines. From his verandah he could hear their cries a mile and a half away. There was only a small body of armed police to block them, he knew. He sent two officers in a motor car to instruct the Police Inspector holding the Mall to use force if necessary to disperse the crowd. There was to be no firing in the air and the police were told to take no risks so far as the safety of women and children were concerned, all of whom were collected and brought to Government House under the protection of a small guard of Indian police.

A large crowd, which had emerged from the Lohari Gate, carrying black flags as a sign of mourning, attempted to force its way along the Anarkali Bazaar and up the Mall, bent on making its way to Government House. It consisted of 10,000 people, formed into a compact mass fifty yards long and twenty deep, howling threats against the whites. The small force of police was steadily pushed back. They were joined by a District Magistrate, Mr Fyson, and the Superintendent of Police, Mr Broadway, and Mr Cocks, Deputy Inspector General of Police. The mob at once attacked these officers and individuals attempted to wrest the weapons from the police, one of whose officers was thrown to the ground, being rescued by his men. Mr Fyson gave the order to fire, twelve to twenty shots being discharged, one of the mob being killed and seven wounded, upon which the crowd fell back. Another mob tried to rush the men of the Royal Sussex Regiment who had arrived in advance of other troops. They met the charge with fixed bayonets and the crowd hesitated and turned back down the Mall.

A contingent of Indian Cavalry arrived to help the exhausted police and the police and troops drove back the rioters, clearing the Mall and the approaches to the Civil Lines, in the process of which the Deputy Superintendent of Police, Mr Clarke, was thrown to the ground by a rioter who jumped on top of him. A constable who raised his rifle to fire at his assailant was stopped by Clarke, who emerged from the encounter unharmed. The police and troops holding the Mall were stoned by rioters on the rooftops for half an hour until, after due warning had been given, they were shot down, suffering three or four casualties, one being fatal.

By 9.30 p.m. the rioters had been driven out of the Mall, but they did not disperse. They gathered in large numbers near the Lohari Gate, from where the efforts of a body of police to dislodge them were unavailing. The cavalry came up and the crowd was slowly pressed back, becoming very dense and estimated by Mr Broadway to number from fifteen to twenty thousand. His men were stoned for half an hour with bricks and on his order, which the Hunter Committee found justified, two or three rounds of buckshot were fired, checking the crowd who, however, remained truculent, turbulent and defiant. When the mob was warned by Mr Fyson that firing would recommence in a few minutes, many people sat down defiantly and more stones were thrown. Quite justifiably, according to the Hunter Committee, Mr Fyson gave another order to fire and some eighteen rioters were wounded, of whom three died subsequently. After this incident the military and police were withdrawn to the Civil Lines, leaving the city in the hands of the rioters, and for two days Lahore was controlled by the mob.

On the morning of the 11th, a crowd of 25,000 Hindus and Muslims, united in common hatred of the Government, paraded in the Badshahi Square, carrying banners which proclaimed 'The king who practises tyranny cuts his roots underneath'. Inflammatory speeches were made, the crowds shouting 'Let us kill the white pigs'. The police firing on the previous day was declared to have been tyrannical and an ex-Sepoy shouted out the false story that the Indian troops in the cantonment had mutinied and were marching on the city. He told his admiring audience that 200 to 250 British soldiers had been killed, adding that he himself had killed six. His announcement was greeted by great enthusiasm by the people, who garlanded him with flowers and carried him shoulder high to a mosque. The crowd then broke up, the people marching through the city crying 'King George is dead' and declaring that the Amir of Afghanistan and the Emperor of Germany were their kings. Another crowd demonstrated outside the fort, tearing down railings and abusing the whites. Persistent attempts were made to bring the railway workers out on strike but the crowd at the locomotive works was dispersed by a force of police armed with guns. Early in the day Sir Michael O'Dwyer invited the political leaders of the Punjab to his house to discuss the situation, thirty to forty attending. Two advised him to parley with the mob, the others stating their opinion that only prompt and drastic action could avert a serious rising. O'Dwyer refused to open negotiations with rebels, feeling that the Government was quite capable of restoring order.

On April 12th another meeting was held outside the Badshahi Mosque at which a number of plain clothes policemen were recognized and attacked, several of them being severely beaten. Colonel Frank Johnson, accompanied by a force of 800 police and soldiers, and supported by two aeroplanes, were sent to regain control of the city. They encountered large crowds sullen and in bad temper on their way and in the square they found a large crowd armed with lathis, which took no notice of warnings to disperse and the people attempted to stampede the cavalry horses. A line of police, led by Mr Fyson, advanced on the dense mass of people, warning them that if they did not disperse they would be fired upon. Upon the crowd closing in behind him and throwing stones, he gave the order to fire and after eight rounds had been fired, the crowd broke, leaving one man killed and twenty-eight wounded, an action which was approved by the Hunter Committee which agreed that the least possible force had been used. That night Sir Michael O'Dwyer spoke on the telephone to the Government of India at Simla, being told, he says, that if troops were forced to fire, 'they should make an example'.

Outbreaks of rioting and mob violence occurred also at Kasur, a town of 25,000 people, twenty-seven miles from Lahore, being occasioned by the news that Gandhi had been kept out of the province and by the news of the disorders at Amritsar, forty miles way. All shops were closed on the 11th, and the *hartal* continued on the 12th, crowds gathering, uttering lamentations and beating their breasts. Those at the railway station worked themselves up into a frenzy, holding up trains and cutting telegraph wires. The train from Ferozepore carrying a number of Europeans was stopped 400 yards from the station. When a white officer appeared at a door, the mob ran to the train shouting, 'Kill him, kill him'. He escaped to a nearby village and a number of women and children passengers took refuge in a hut where they were attacked by the mob, being saved by the gallant action of Khan Din, a railway inspector, who stoutly defended them. The train was driven into the station where two white warrant officers, armed with revolvers, were pelted with stones by the crowd as they stood at the door of their compartment. They made the mistake of discharging their revolvers at too great a distance and the crowd closed in. The warrant officers attempted to escape by running down the platform; they were caught and killed. The mob burned the station and other mobs attacked the Court House and Treasury from where they were driven off by armed police, fifty-seven shots being fired, killing four rioters, an action upheld by the Hunter Committee.

In many places in the Punjab trains were stopped, derailed and the railway lines were torn up and telegraph wires cut, which, according to Sir Michael O'Dwyer, was part of a pre-arranged design to immobilize troops and isolate the main centres of rebellion. To prove that these 'persistent' attacks on railways and telegraph lines were part of the rebels' plan of campaign, the significance of which, he says, was not apprehended by the Hunter Committee of Enquiry, he cites the example of the Indian railway signaller at Lahore who, on April 10th, sent messages to his friends at Delhi that Lahore was being looted, the Indian troops were about to rise and the railway workers were about to strike, and urging them to do the same. On April 12th a message was signalled from Delhi to railway workers 'after consultation with the leaders of the agitation at Delhi' that, on receiving the word 'Rowlatt', they were to do the 'needful' at once. A railway strike would, O'Dwyer says, have made it impossible to move troops to crush the rapidly spreading rebellion. He states that there were 132 cases of tearing up rails, looting stations and cutting telegraph wires in nineteen of the twenty-nine Districts of the Punjab.

Both Sir Michael O'Dwyer and General Dyer maintained that the disturbances in the Punjab were part of a well-organized rebellion intended to kick the British out of India, a view which was not shared by the Hunter Committee which investigated the 'Disorders in the Punjab'.

Meanwhile General Dyer had arrived back at his headquarters at Jullundur on April 6th, being met by Captain Briggs with the news that a code message had been received on the previous day from the Divisional Commander at Lahore, warning that trouble might be expected over the Rowlatt Acts and ordering General Dyer to get in touch with Amritsar and stressing 'special precautions Amritsar'. Captain Briggs informed him that he had been in consultation with the military commander in that city who, he learned, was 'in touch with the civil authorities and aware of the possibility of trouble'. On further orders from Lahore, Dyer dispatched an Indian officer and twenty Sepoys as a guard for the railway station at Amritsar. In Jullundur, April 6th and the next three days passed off quietly. Then, at 4 p.m. on the 10th, General Dyer received a code message from Amritsar, urgently asking for British troops, guns and an aeroplane.

IV

FLARE UP IN AMRITSAR

The *hartal* in Amritsar, a city of 150,000 people, twenty miles from Lahore, on March 30th passed off quietly. It was entirely successful and all business was stopped; there were no clashes. On the previous day an order had been served on the local Home Rule leader, a physician and surgeon, Dr Satyapal, forbidding him to speak in public, and on April 4th similar injunctions were imposed on two other leaders, Dr Saif-ud-din Kitchlew, a barrister who is described as 'an extremist and home ruler of pronounced anti-government views', and Pandit Kotu Mal, a member of the Congress Party. One of Gandhi's followers, Swami Satya Deo, however, was allowed to deliver a lecture on 'Soul Force', as he tried to dissuade people from violence and from holding meetings until Gandhi called on them to go to jail in thousands. The disturbances at Delhi on March 30th seem at first to have discouraged the local Congress Committee from declaring a further *hartal* in Amritsar on April 6th, but at a private meeting held on the evening of the 5th, at which both Dr Satyapal and Dr Kitchlew were present, it was decided to proceed.

The second *hartal* passed off quietly, Europeans being permitted to walk about unmolested, and the organizers, Doctors Satyapal and Kitchlew, in the words of the Deputy Commissioner, refrained from any overt act of intimidation which could justify intervention. But a poster was found exhibited on the Clock Tower calling on the people of Amritsar to 'die and kill'. An Englishwoman, of whom we shall hear more later, found the attitude of shopkeepers at this time distinctly unfriendly.

The situation, however, had begun to take on threatening aspects, says Mr Miles Irving, the Deputy Commissioner, in his written statement prepared for the Hunter Committee. While the intention of the brains behind the movement was to avoid violence, he believed, they had raised a storm which had got beyond their control. Their intention was, he thought, to organize passive resistance which would paralyze the govern-

3
Left: The Kucha Kaurianwala (the Crawling Lane) where Miss Sherwood was attacked

Right: Where Miss Sherwood took shelter is shown by the boy in the foreground

4
Above: The National Bank at Amritsar after the rioting

Below: The Alliance Bank at Amritsar: the room where Mr Thompson was murdered

ment, and avoid any collision with the authorities which would justify armed intervention. He was much perturbed by the proof, afforded by the second *hartal*, of the power and influence of Doctors Satyapal and Kitchlew, and on April 8th he wrote to the Punjab Government pointing out that from one cause or another the people of Amritsar were restless and discontented, and he pressed urgently for an increase in the military forces, stating his opinion that with the existing garrison any resolute action in the city would leave the Civil Lines undefended. If a riot occurred 'we must abandon nine-tenths of the city, holding only the Kotwali (the chief police station) and communications', he stated, adding 'even so we will be hard pressed to defend the station and Civil Lines'. The *hartal*, in his view, was a mere step to test the organization. Who were behind it, he could not say. The Congress Committee came to heel when Dr Kitchlew ordered it, he said, and he described him as 'the local agent of very much bigger men'. He went on to tell the Provincial Government 'I was wrong in thinking I could influence Kitchlew—he is too deep in', and he stated 'I think that things will be worse before they are better and that for the present we must rely on ourselves alone'.

The next three days in Amritsar passed without incident. On the evening of the 9th the Hindu festival of *Ram Naumi* was observed, the only disquieting feature being that it was celebrated by Hindus and Muslims alike, a sinister example of religious fraternization which boded ill for the traditional British policy of 'divide and rule'. Water, says Mr Miles Irving, was provided by Muslims and drunk from their hands by Hindus, although he took some comfort from the fact that silver drinking vessels were used. The sinister co-operation of the two opposing religious factions was further exemplified by a cricket match played between the Muslim club and the Hindu Sabha which, according to Khwaja Yusuf Shah, a Municipal Commissioner and a member of the Provincial Legislative Council, caused great rivalry and led to 'bitter feelings', which may have given some comfort to the British. The Hunter Committee found that the festival became a striking demonstration in furtherance of Hindu-Muslim unity, and, as the procession passed through the streets, the cries raised, instead of those giving honour to Hindu deities, were of political import. But there was little sign of active hostility to the government and none to Europeans as such, Mr Irving found. A reassuring state of affairs of which he himself

D

experienced a striking example as he watched the procession unguarded from the verandah of the Allahabad Bank. Every car in the procession stopped in front of him and the accompanying band played *God Save the King*. The only note of disloyalty that struck Mr Irving was that a party of Muslim students, dressed to represent Turkish soldiers, Britain's late enemies, raised a demonstration by clapping their hands, which he found to be a sign of rudeness. Lala Jiwan Lal, a C.I.D. officer, who mingled with the crowds, on the other hand, overheard remarks derogatory to the government, people crying, he told the Hunter Committee, 'dust be on the heads of those that flatter the Government'.

The order which was to precipitate violence in Amritsar next day had already been decided upon, one which, according to Mr Jayakar of the Congress Sub-Committee of Enquiry, 'added fuel to the fire'. When Mr Irving returned to his bungalow from watching the procession, he found an order had arrived from the Provincial Government instructing him to deport Doctors Satyapal and Kitchlew quietly to Dharmsala in another part of the province, and a letter informing him that his request for reinforcements had been passed on to the General Officer Commanding Division in Lahore with the statement that 'the Lieutenant-Governor agrees with Mr Irving that the military garrison at Amritsar requires strengthening as early as possible'.

Although the situation did not seem to argue any serious results from the arrest of the two local leaders, Mr Irving decided to take steps to prevent any disorderly demonstrations which might result, or any attempt to rescue the deportees. He called a conference consisting of himself, the Superintendent of Police, Mr J. F. Rehill, Mr R. Plomer, his deputy, the Officer Commanding the troops in the city, Captain J. W. Massey, and Colonel Henry Smith, the Civil Surgeon, at which it was decided that Doctors Satyapal and Kitchlew should be invited to the Deputy Commissioner's bungalow at 10 a.m. next day, when they would immediately be arrested, placed in a motor car in the charge of Mr Rehill and driven away, Captain Massey's suggestion being adopted that he should provide a British military escort in another car, the four soldiers being disguised to look as though they were going out on a shooting party. Arrangements were made for a picket of soldiers to be present at the bungalow to overawe any crowd who might make a demonstration, and for further parties to picket the three bridges over the railway line which separated the city from the Civil Lines. The rest of the British infantry would be kept in reserve in the Ram Bagh Gardens and seventy-five armed police were to be stationed in the chief police post in the city, the Kotwali, the remainder of police being positioned at the railway level crossing. If trouble arose, Colonel Smith would take his motor ambulance into the city to evacuate the white women and children. Returning to his cantonment that night, Captain Massey called on the European bank officials, warning them of the impending arrests and advising them to come out of the city, a timely though unofficial warning that went unheeded. That night Mr Irving issued orders to three European Magistrates to post themselves next day at the three railway bridges to prevent any body exceeding five persons from crossing the line. They were told to keep the crowd back, peacefully if possible, but if necessary by military force.

Early next morning Captain Massey placed ninety of his men, fifty mounted men belonging to No. 12 Ammunition Column, Royal Artillery, and forty men of the Somerset Light Infantry, in the Ram Bagh Gardens, an open space between the city and the railway line. This, according to the evidence given to the Hunter Committee, left him with some 180 infantrymen to dispose of elsewhere which, together with the small picket of Indian troops which had been sent from Jullundur to guard the station, composed the effective garrison of Amritsar, of which only thirty were white men. Captain Massey took Captain Botting, who was in charge of the ammuition column, round the various posts which had been selected and showed him where to place pickets at the railway bridges and crossings and he warned the officer commanding at the fort to be ready to cover the evacuation of white women and children with his machine guns. He was not to hesitate to fire if the mob attacked the fort, he was instructed. At 9.45 a.m. Captain Massey arrived at the Deputy Commissioner's bungalow with a picket composed of men of the Somerset Light Infantry, stationing them discreetly behind the Court House.

These arrangements, 'The Internal Defence Scheme' for protecting the Civil Lines, the European quarter, were, the Hunter Committee observes, sufficiently elaborate to suggest very grave apprehension in the Deputy Commissioner's mind as regarding the consequence of carrying out the deportations, but the Committee found that no one on the night of the 9th anticipated, or had any reason to anticipate, that next day would see disorders as grave as those which in fact took place. The Committee observed that, whilst it was a matter of great regret that no steps were taken officially to warn Europeans not to go into the city as usual, it could not have been anticipated that a murderous antipathy towards all Europeans would break out next day.

The map of Amritsar on page 12, which was printed by the Hunter Committee with its Report, shows the location of the serious disorders which broke out so suddenly and unexpectedly on April 10th. Readers will observe that the railway line, the scene of the initial clashes, lies to the north-west of the city, dividing it from the European quarter, the Ram Bagh Gardens and the Gobina Garh Fort marking the extremities of the area in which the collisions occurred.

At 8 a.m. Dr Satyapal received a note from Mr Miles Irving inviting him to come to his house at 10 a.m. and, not attaching much importance to it, he went on his daily rounds, reaching the house at about five or ten minutes to ten, where, a few minutes later, Dr Kitchlew arrived also. After being kept waiting for some minutes in a tent pitched outside, they were taken into the house, into a room in which were Mr Irving, Mr Rehill and Mr Beckett, the Assistant Commissioner. The Orders issued by the Punjab Government under the Defence of India Act were placed in their hands and they were asked to leave Amritsar at once. They were put in separate motor cars which drove off at high speed, the military escort accompanying them as far as Shahpur.

The deportation of the two local leaders did not go unnoticed for several of their friends had accompanied them to the Deputy Commissioner's bungalow. These people were detained for half an hour, to give the cortege a good start, and they were then allowed to return to the city, Captain Massey leaving at the same time and riding back to the Ram Bagh.

At 11 a.m. Mr Plomer, the Deputy-Superintendent of Police, received a telephone message from the Inspector in charge of the Kotwali saying that mobs were on the move and they were making their way to Aitchison Park and assembling with the intention of demanding the release of the deportees. The mob, he was told, was under the leadership of two local hooligans, Bugga and Ratto, one of whom owned a gambling den, the other being a gang leader, who had a lot of riff-raff with them. Both men had influence with the mob, Mr Plomer was warned. He immediately telephoned the Deputy Commissioner to that effect.

Section Eleven of the Hunter Committee Majority Report describes the demeanour and behaviour of the crowd at this early stage:

'About 11.30, however, the news of the deportation was spreading in the city: shops were being closed on all sides and crowds were collecting. A large crowd formed in Hall Bazaar and made its way through Hall Gate and over the Hall Bridge at the further side of which was a small picquet of mounted troops. This crowd was excited and angry at the deportations and was undoubtedly making for the civil lines bent upon seeing the Deputy Commissioner. A Criminal Investigation Department Inspector who gave evidence before us and whom we believe, states that he was in the back portion of this crowd on the first slope of the road bridge and that members of the crowd near him as they were going over the bridge and before they had been fired upon or turned back, were crying out, "Where is the Deputy Commissioner? We will butcher him to pieces." Another witness, Dr Muhammad Abdullah Fauq, states that he was with this crowd and that the cries were that they must see the Deputy Commissioner, ask him where these leaders were, and if he would not grant their release, insist on themselves also being taken to the same place. It is an ascertained fact that this angry crowd as it poured out of the city towards the bridge took no notice of Europeans whom it met on the way. Mr Jarman, the Municipal Engineer, passed it by and was not molested. There is on the evidence very slender ground for supposing that this crowd in its initial stages was possessed of, or by, any definite common intention save that of angry and obstreperous protest in force before the Deputy Commissioner at his house and for the purpose of overawing him. It was as events showed equal to anything but had not as yet resolved upon anything very definite. Violent and excited threats against the Deputy Commissioner we think there were, but it is not certain that these were many or that they were representative in the first phase of the disturbance. The mob had not armed themselves with sticks or *lathis*. Still it is abundantly clear that the crowd was not a mere crowd of mourning and that to represent it as a large but peaceful body bent on respectful, or even lawful, protest before authority is a travesty of facts. We consider that the Deputy Commissioner was right, and had done no more than his duty, when he resolved to prevent entry into the civil lines by any such crowd. Beyond this it remains undeniable of this particular crowd that it was likely to cause a disturbance of the public peace and that public security was manifestly endangered by it.'

Instructing Mr Plomer to warn Captain Massey, Mr Miles Irving rode at once to the Hall Gate Bridge over the railway.

Captain Massey, from his position in the Ram Bagh Gardens, saw a vast crowd debouching from the city. He at once dispatched his mounted men to strengthen the pickets holding the bridges over the railway and he went himself to the railway station, setting guards at the Telegraph Office and at the footbridge. Mr Plomer, the Assistant Superintendent of Police, who galloped up, told him that the mob was breaking out of the city in thousands and making for the Commissioner's bungalow. Leaving the railway station, Captain Massey hurried to the Hall Gate Bridge, from where he saw a roaring crowd surging out of the city, howling like madmen and, in his opinion, absolutely out of control.

Mr R. B. Beckett, the Assistant Commissioner who had been appointed to act as a Magistrate, proceeded to his station at the Hall Gate Bridge. When he turned the corner about 1 p.m. he heard a noise 'like the noise of the sea'. He stuck his heels into his horse and galloped as hard as he could. At the foot of the bridge stood four mounted soldiers, and four infantry men had placed themselves on the ironwork of the bridge. In front of them, only about eight to ten yards away, stood a vast crowd, numbering, it was afterwards estimated, 30,000 people, stretching as far as he could see and continually increasing. They were shouting and behaving in a most fanatical manner, making faces and waving their arms. Three men were running about in front of the crowd. Taking with him the four infantry men, only two of whom were armed with rifles, Mr Beckett went towards the crowd, shouting and gesticulating for them to go back, but he could not make himself heard. The people howled him down and advanced in a threatening manner. They were, in his opinion, intensely excited and bent on mischief and they were not amenable to persuasion.

Lala Gian Chand, who had closed his trunk shop, was a member of the crowd which assembled at the bridge. In front of it he saw the Assistant Commissioner on horseback and wearing a white suit; with him were three or four mounted Europeans and an Indian Muslim military man, also on horseback, carrying a lance. The Europeans, he saw, had rifles in their hands, except the man in white, who was carrying only a hunting crop. The crowd, he told the Congress Sub-Committee, were unarmed and bareheaded. When the Commissioner asked them to go back, many of them sat down and beat their breasts. Some of the crowd advanced towards the horseman and had some talk with him, but he could not hear what was said. The horses, he noticed, were getting restless and the man in white appeared to be waving the crowd back. But no one listened to him. The crowd advanced, the horsemen being pushed back, people starting to clap their hands.

Finding it impossible to hold the crowd back, Mr Beckett told the N.C.O. in charge of the four white soldiers, 'We have got to keep this crowd from crossing the bridge and you have got to do all in your power to prevent them from doing so'. The crowd pressed forward, driving the soldiers over the bridge and down the road on the other side, hitting the horses which became 'absolutely frantic', according to Mr Beckett. He managed to keep his horse with its head facing the crowd but the other four were, he saw, absolutely out of control. A man came up and hit his horse on the nose with a small cane, making it turn about. Beckett was forced to follow the soldiers, the crowd pressing in around and behind them. He tried to rally his men but the horses refused to face the crowd. This was the situation when Mr Miles Irving rode up. Captain Massey, who was endeavouring to make his way to the Ram Bagh to bring up reinforcements, was cut off by the crowd and he was forced to make a detour on which, through some misunderstanding, he was joined by the infantry picket which had been held in reserve.

The crowd found a pile of bricks beside the road and, picking them up, they started to stone Beckett and his men, one of whom fired his rifle in the air without effect, according to official evidence. Lala Gian Chand, however, says that one horseman fired two shots, striking two persons, upon which the crowd fell back. The wounded men, he says, were carried to Dr Bashir's house in the Farid Bazaar.

Mr F. A. Connor, an Extra Assistant Commissioner, reached the scene of the disturbance soon after 1 p.m., encountering a mounted picket which was trotting back from the bridge at a very fast pace, being stoned by a large and very dense crowd. Its commander, Lieutenant Dickie, seeing Connor, called out, 'For

God's sake send some reinforcements'. Realizing that Dickie and his men were in very serious peril, Connor called out that it was up to him to fire on the mob as it was his duty to protect the Civil Lines. Dickie, who said he was glad to have the order, dismounted two of his men who, taking cover behind some culverts, fired five or six shots which brought the crowd to a dead standstill. The Hunter Committee found this firing completely justified and 'absolutely necessary' in the circumstances and in no way exceeding the occasion.

The angry people, reports Connor, made a murderous yell, quite unlike their usual cry. Two men he spoke to demanded the release of Satyapal and Kitchlew, one man striking his chest and saying they should have the two men back or they were willing to die. The other man told Connor that the British had offered them self-government and were giving them bullets. The firing had the desired effect, the crowd pouring back so that only these two men were left on the road, says Connor.

At this stage Mr Plomer, the Deputy Superintendent of Police, arrived with thirty armed policemen and two pony-cart loads of Somerset Light Infantry men, who were lined up along the railway line. Some local lawyers approached Mr Miles Irving, asking to be allowed to try to induce the crowd, which was streaming away, to return to the city, and they were permitted to do so. The danger remained; the crowd might try again to cross the Civil Lines, realized Mr Irving. Returning to his bungalow he tried to telephone to Lahore, but the line had been cut. He dispatched an officer on a light engine to go down the railway line in order to reach the uncut wire and send a telegram to the Officer Commanding the 16th Division, requesting reinforcements.

The crowd which had been prevented from reaching the Commissioner's bungalow was now, in the words of Mr Jayakar, 'no longer a peaceful crowd, but a crowd foiled in its efforts to secure the release of its leaders and exasperated at the killing and wounding of its members'. Enraged, and with its feelings beyond control, carrying with it the killed and wounded men, the crowd streamed back towards the railway station and the city. The white officials standing on the bridge saw flames and dense smoke rising above the rooftops of Amritsar.

Colonel Henry Smith, the Civil Surgeon, was engaged in an operation for cataract in the Jubilee Hospital, when his assistant called to him, 'They are firing, sir'. Finishing the operation which only took a minute, Smith picked up the telephone to speak to the Deputy Commissioner but the line was dead. Realizing the need to evacuate the women missionaries from the city, Smith took his motor ambulance to the Mission Hospital where, leaving his driver at the wheel with the engine running, he dashed inside and ordered the three white women to go to the ambulance. They assured him they would not be molested and they said they would stay. Smith told them he had not come to discuss matters. His orders were to evacuate them and he got the three women and some thirty to forty Indian Christian women into the ambulance, driving them out of the city, passing on the way one of the Mission Schools, which was burning. He took the refugees to the rallying point arranged at one of the canal bungalows inside the Civil Lines.

In this bungalow was living an Englishwoman who tells us that she had just lain down under the punkah at one o'clock when the servant came to say that a lady wished to see her. She tells the story of her experiences in Amritsar on that memorable day:

'I rose reluctantly, annoyed with my bearer for having admitted a visitor after my order that I was not to be disturbed; but before I could leave the room a second knock announced the arrival of more visitors, and my bearer poured forth a long story, of which the only words I could catch were "Badmash" (scoundrels) and "Bazaar". His voice was drowned by the shrill cries of babies in the next room, and it flashed upon my memory that the house had been chosen as a rallying-post for European women and children in the event of trouble. My suspicions were quickly confirmed when I came into a drawing-room full of people I had never seen before, who paid no attention whatever to my entry. Fresh arrivals poured in every minute, and from one or two acquaintances among them I elicited the little that they knew of what had happened. A few minutes earlier a wild crowd had burst over the Hall Bridge driving back and stoning the small picket which was posted there. No shots had then been fired, but the howl of the mob could be heard a quarter of a mile away, and the residents in the main thoroughfare were rapidly warned to leave their bungalows for the rallying-posts. The crowd was close at hand, and a moment's delay might prove fatal; but at this somnolent hour it was no small task to persuade the women to move, and one of them persistently refused to quit her house because her baby was asleep. As people left their bungalows a few shots were heard from the direction of the bridge, but nothing was known then of the course of events. From men passing on horseback we gradually learned a few details, and before long we saw smoke and flames rising from the city and heard that Europeans were being murdered.'

Two British women who had remained in the city had fortunate escapes, but one of them was brutally attacked. Mrs Isabel Mary Easdon, a doctor at the Zenana Hospital, warned that a crowd was collecting outside, unwisely showed herself on the roof where, according to Indians present, she made provocative remarks, being reported to have said that those who had been killed had got what they deserved. The mob shouted for her to be thrown down, and when she disappeared they stormed the hospital gate and rushed up the stairs. Mrs Easdon's assistant took her to the room of assistant surgeon Mrs Nelly Benjamin, who hid her in a closet, swearing to the searchers on her bended knees that Mrs Easdon had left the hospital. Mrs Easdon, crouching in her hiding place only a yard away, heard the disappointed cries of her would-be assailants. When the crowd left she was smuggled out in disguise and taken to the house of a police constable. Miss Marcella Sherwood, a lady missionary, the Superintendent of the City Mission Schools, was bicycling to one of her schools when she was spotted and pursued by a mob which intercepted her in the Kucha Kaurianwala, a narrow lane. She got up to run and succeeded in reaching a house, the door of which was slammed in her face. Beaten down again she was left for dead in the street and she was later picked up by the father of one of her Hindu girls, who hid her until evening.

Several other Europeans in the city were attacked and some of them were murdered. Enraged crowds looted and burnt the National Bank, killing Mr Stewart, the manager, and Mr Scott, his assistant, burning their bodies on a pile of furniture soaked with kerosene. The Alliance Bank was attacked, its manager, Mr G. M. Thompson, who attempted to defend himself with a revolver, being flung from the balcony into the street where his body was burnt under a pile of bank furniture drenched with kerosene. The building itself was not destroyed, presumably, the Hunter Committee found, because it was owned by Indians. The manager of the Chartered Bank, Mr J. W. Thompson, and his assistant, Mr Ross, were hidden in an upper storey by their clerks and later rescued by a posse of police from the neighbouring Kotwali, but under circumstances that did the police officer in charge little credit.

All three banks were situated within three hundred yards of the Kotwali, yet the seventy-five armed policemen and twenty-five detectives stationed there under two officers, Khan Sahib Ahmad Jan, Deputy Superintendent with thirty years' service, and Muhammed Ashraf Khan, City Inspector with twenty-five years' service, made no attempt to prevent the mob outrages at the bank and they allowed the Town Hall, which adjoined the Kotwali, to be burnt down under their noses. The ineffective handling of the police at the Kotwali and the futile efforts of the Deputy Superintendent, who took a party to the Chartered Bank, were severely criticized by the Hunter Committee, who found that the evidence given by the two officers conflicted on material points.

The lack of initiative displayed by the police arose, it seems, from personal animosity between the two officers, from confusing orders and ill-defined seniority. Both officers stated that the other was in charge; Ashraf Khan being 'City' Inspector and Sahib Ahmad Jan, Deputy Superintendent of the 'rural' area. As a result they acted, or failed to act, independently and nothing was done to prevent either the outrage at the banks or the burning of the Town Hall.

Excited crowds started to pass the Kotwali about 12.30 p.m., heading out of the city, shouting for the release of Satyapal and Kitchelew and calling for Hindu-Muslim unity. Firing was heard from the railway lines and the crowd streamed back into the city. No attempt was made by the police to stop them or overawe them, and the two officers at the Kotwali were entirely unaware of the attacks on the banks, or that a mob was setting fire to the Town Hall, until some clerks on the roof of the Chartered Bank, fifty yards away, were seen waving and shouting. While Sahib Ahmad Jan took a party of twenty-five armed police to the Chartered Bank, Ashraf Khan rescued Mr Jarman, the Municipal Engineer, from the Town Hall.

When the Deputy Superintendent reached the Chartered Bank, he found it surrounded by a mob of 2,000 rioters, some of whom had already got inside. He forced his way in, dispersing the crowd, and rescued the manager, Mr J. W. Thompson, and his assistant, Mr Ross, who had been hidden by their clerks. So far so good. But, instead of returning to the Kotwali, Ahmad

Jan remained in the deserted bank, dispatching Messrs Thompson and Ross to the Kotwali under escort, until 5 p.m. He knew nothing, he told the Hunter Committee, of the attacks on the other banks, and when he was asked if he did not think that something 'unruly and unusual' was going on in the city, and that similar incidents might be taking place elsewhere, he replied, 'I couldn't think that' and 'It did not strike me'. He thought he was doing his duty by remaining at the Chartered Bank. He stayed there, he said, after the two Europeans had been smuggled out, to give the impression they were still there so that the mob would not assault the Kotwali. In order to distract the rioters further he walked up the road to within thirty yards of the police station, but he didn't enter it, nor did it strike him that anything unusual was happening. Meanwhile, at the Kotwali, according to Inspector Ashraf Khan, he sent out a party of police to the Alliance and National Banks, which left him only twenty-five men with which to protect the police station. The police, sent too late to protect the banks, made a half-hearted demonstration, threatening to fire but not doing so, learned Mr C. G. Farquhar, Deputy Inspector-General of Police, who came to Amritsar to investigate the failure of the native police to protect the whites in the city.

Considering the matter, the Hunter Committee attributed the failure of the police to grasp the situation to 'their lack of initiative'. Its report states, 'Seventy-five armed men, handled with ordinary skill and alertness, could have made impossible the outrages which took place close to the Kotwali, and it called the Deputy Inspector's conduct at the Chartered Bank 'pointless and ineffective beyond excuse'.

Due to the inactivity of the police, the Committee found, the mobs in the city were left uncontrolled, one of them catching Sergeant Rowlands, Electrician to the Military Works, on his way out of the city, bludgeoning him to death, a murder which brought the European death roll inside the city to four, a number further increased by the killing of a railway guard named Robinson at the goods yard, a point to which we can now return. Other mobs in the city burnt down the Religious Book Society's hall, an Indian Christian church, a school and three sub-post offices.

The mob, 30,000 strong, which had been forced back from the railway crossings, scattered in all directions, bent on violence, in the words of Mr Miles Irving. Some of the rioters rushed back into the city; others turned aside to attack the railway goods yard and the telegraph office.

Early in the morning Captain Massey had strengthened the guard at the railway station, but the events at the bridge had necessitated the withdrawal of the picket commanded by Lieutenant Browne, leaving a dangerous situation which was unexpectedly relieved by the arrival by train of 260 unarmed Gurkhas en route for Peshawar, under the command of Captain Crampton, who agreed to break his journey, and a hundred of his men were equipped with rifles from the fort. But despite these additional guards a mob rushed the telegraph office, smashing instruments and killing Robinson, who was armed only with an umbrella. 'When the mob had done with him, he bore no resemblance to a human being. He was simply a bundle of red rags', Captain John Botting said in 1924. They were on the point of killing Mr Bennett, the Telegraph Master, when a picket commanded by Subedar Zardad Khan came up from the station and drove off his assailants at the point of the bayonet and dispersed the crowd by firing eighteen rounds. Lala Jiwan Lal, the C.I.D. Inspector who was present, heard the mob shouting, 'they killed our brethren and we shall kill them'. He found the situation so dangerous, he told the Hunter Committee, that he left the place and went home. Mr Plomer noticed that the mob had armed themselves with *lathis* and railings, and they were brandishing them about. By 2 p.m. all telegraph and telephone wires out of Amritsar had been cut, and during the afternoon several railway goods yards were looted and trains derailed in the district.

While these incidents were taking place within the city and at the railway goods yard, other rioters made a second attempt to cross the railway lines. Mr Miles Irving and Mr Plomer saw a huge crowd approaching the bridge. Taking some mounted men with them the two officials rode towards the crowd and endeavoured to make them disperse, an object in which they were assisted by two Indian lawyers, Maqbool Mahmood and Gurdial Singh Salaria, who placed themselves between the mob and the soldiers, waving and shouting for both sides to go back and for the soldiers to hold their fire. Mr Salaria told the Congress Sub-Committee that some of the crowd agreed to disperse if they were given the bodies of their brethren who had been shot down. Feeling himself unable to reach the crowd effectively on foot, he asked for and was provided with a horse by Mr Plomer, riding in amongst the crowd and appealing for them to go back. The crowd was very much excited and were shouting, he says. Some of the mob threw sticks at the Deputy Commissioner, who was reluctant to give orders to fire in case the lawyers might be hit. But according to Mr Salaria, the soldiers began to fire without warning. He and his friends were saved only by a miracle. Maqbool Mahmood told the Sub-Committee: 'After the first few shots, the crowd rushed back, but the firing was continued even after they began running away. Many of them were hit on the back. Most of the wounded were hit above the belt, on the face or on the head. From what I saw there myself, I have no hesitation in saying that such firing as was resorted to was unnecessary. The crowd could have been effectively dispersed without any firing or in any event by a few shots aimed at their legs.'

The Hunter Committee Report records that twenty or thirty casualties ensued and it observes 'at this stage, and of this crowd, we consider it certain that the temper and the determination to do violence was more obvious, more resolute and more vicious than that which had been exhibited earlier in the day. We think that the order to fire was rightly given and we can find no grounds for saying that the necessity of the moment was in any way exceeded or abused.'

Maqbool Mahmood relates:

'It was by mere accident that our lives were saved. I still believe if the authorities had a little more patience, we would have succeeded in taking the crowd back. It is a matter of regret that when the authorities decided to fire, they did not make any arrangement or an ambulance car or first aid. I believe some of the wounded might have been saved if timely medical assistance had been forthcoming.

'I witnessed many pathetic scenes and some gruesome sights. I saw a corpse actually with an eyeball and the whole brain blown out. I heard a dying man gasping, "Hindu Mussalmanki jai". One incident is particularly noteworthy. A boy of sixteen or seventeen years of age lay wounded with his entrails protruding, having been hit on the belly. When Dr Dhanpat Rai, Salaria and I approached him, he whispered, "I am dying, don't trouble about me, attend to my brethren. Hindu Mussalmanki jai." The next moment he died. Many similar instances of notable sacrifice I noticed when I was pouring water into the mouths of the dying.'

The mob, which Captain Massey estimated to number 40,000, went back into the city crying and shouting, 'Innocent people have been shot', as Dr Bal Mukund, an assistant surgeon at the hospital, heard it. By 3 p.m., when Mr Miles Irving was informed of the incendiarism in the city, all was quiet outside. A number of rioters had been killed and wounded, entirely justifiably according to the Hunter Committee. The Congress Sub-Committee, on the other hand, while it granted that the crowd was in an 'assertive mood', recorded its opinion that there was 'no warrant for the firing'. The authorities, it declared, had omitted the usual stages. There had been no parleying, no humouring, no use of milder force. The mob had not indulged in excesses and there was no occasion for impatience.

Our Englishwoman records:

'The afternoon passed slowly, with rumours and alarms which increased the suspense of the many women who did not know where their husbands were. Those of us who had anything to do were too busy to think, and three of the women and three of the babies were ill; but human nature is always the same, and I was amused to see on returning to my room that my dressing-table had been depleted of everything that could be used as a cosmetic, as if a horde of locusts had settled on it, and we had to make peace between one or two who "could not sit under a punkah" and the majority who were prepared to faint if it was turned off.'

At 5 p.m., Mr A. J. W. Kitchin, the Commissioner at Lahore, and the Deputy Inspector General of Police for the Punjab, Central Range, Mr C. G. Farquhar, reached Amritsar by car, having received Mr Irving's telegram at 1.30 p.m. General Dyer had been ordered to send 400 men from Jullundur that night, Irving was told. There was still no definite news of the position within the city; rumours said that the police force at the Kotwali had been wiped out but that there were still some Europeans alive in the city. Asked if he could spare a striking force to enter the city, Captain Massey stated that his small force was not strong enough to do so as well as protect the Civil Lines, and the railway, and cover the evacuation of women and children to the Fort. But it might be possible to do so after nightfall, he thought, when the expected reinforcements arrived. The tension was relieved by the news that the Europeans in the Kotwali were in no danger. The safety of the women and children was the first concern, Captain Massey told the conference of officials, and for an account of this operation we turn to our anonymous Englishwoman:

'About half an hour before sunset, news came that the Fort was ready to receive us. Every possible conveyance had been secured, and we packed ourselves in, making a picture like Epsom road on the Derby Day. Very few had brought anything with them, so we stripped the house of everything that could be used as bedding during the coming night.

'The Fort of Gobindgarh, which we were now to know so well, was built over a hundred years ago by the great Maharaja Ranjit Singh, to protect the treasure which he kept with the bankers of Amritsar, prosperous then as now. It is said that he employed an Italian engineer, and traces of its exotic origin linger in the names of the different blocks and passages. To reach the Fort, we had to cross the railway line, which our handful of troops had held all day against the hordes from the city, by the Rego bridge. We set forth with some trepidation; but the arrival of some Gurkha troops about this time enabled the road to be picketed, and the way was safe. Men from the Central Followers' Depot, armed with staves, accompanied us, and it was not long before we were driving through the winding entrances to the Fort.

'Dusk was now falling, and we had to make haste to prepare for the night. We found places where we could, and most of us packed into the upper storey of the "Cavalier Block", which rises in the centre of the great quadrangle. The heat, however, was stifling. There were not half a dozen fans in the whole Fort, including those in the hospital and the canteen hall, and many people found it the lesser of two evils to spend the night on the ground outside. One or two had managed to get their bedding brought in by their servants, but the rest were ill-equipped for the conditions they had to face. We distributed the heavy clothing, blankets, and rugs which we had brought from the bungalow, but there would not have been enough to go round if the garrison had not given up some of their blankets. Our next thought was to find a meal for the many women and children who had eaten nothing since early morning. We had only the scraps which we had brought away from the bungalow, but once again the soldiers came to our rescue and gave up half their bread ration. All these things were being done at once, amid indescribable turmoil.

'A roll-call revealed 130 women and children, besides babies; the civilian men who were not too old or sick had already been posted to defence duties round the Fort and made up another fifty. A number of servants also had come down before the gates of the Fort closed at sundown, and presented another problem, as they required native food. While they were being given their handfuls of grain to last them till the morning, a grey-bearded old Sikh orderly, Sher Singh, proudly refused to take his share, saying he had often gone without food for two or three days on the field of battle. This man set a splendid example throughout, and indeed all the servants behaved well under very trying circumstances.'

The train bringing the 400 men, 175 Baluchis and 125 Royal Sussex Regiment, commanded by Major MacDonald, reached Amritsar at 11 p.m. That officer was told by Mr Kitchin that the situation was beyond civil control and that he, as senior military officer, should take such steps as the military situation demanded, and he was advised that he should take his troops into the city to rescue the Europeans at the Kotwali. Major MacDonald went at once, Mr Kitchin refraining from sending a Civil Officer with him, as he did not wish to embarrass Major MacDonald with the presence of a civil officer senior to himself.

Major MacDonald marched to the Kotwali and returned, bringing out the four Europeans hiding there, Mr J. W. Thompson, Mr Ross, Mr Jarman and Sergeant Parsonage, and rescuing also Mrs Easdon and Miss Sherwood, who was so badly injured that she lay at the Fort, swathed in bandages for nineteen days before she could be moved.

For the story of that night in Amritsar we return to our Englishwoman:

'It had long been dark, and we were still working hard to get things straight and settle people down for the night, when I was suddenly drawn away by an officer, who whispered a request for a lantern in order to bring in what was left of Mr Thompson's body from one of the banks. Desperately afraid lest this news should spread, I secured the only lantern in the Fort for him, and he went away. We afterwards heard that this was the body of Sergeant Rawlings, which had just been found, beaten to death, beneath the walls of the Fort, and not Mr Thompson's, which had not then been recovered. When nothing more was left to be done, some of us went on to the ramparts for a few minutes' quiet, and from the top of the western wall we saw the native city ablaze with electric light—a contrast to the darkness behind us.

'At midnight we turned in, but daylight seemed to come before we had closed our eyes. The outlook was not pleasant for women who had never known a day's real hardship before; they found themselves suddenly stripped of all the decencies and comforts they had come to look upon as necessities, and surrounded by the miseries of dirt, heat, and overcrowding. There was no sanitation; everything depended on the servants, who had not yet been organized. There was no privacy, and we had to hide under our bedding to dress ourselves. Sixteen people shared one small room for the first three days, and those who had no rooms were really better off. There were no beds, no proper bedding, no mosquito-nets, no fans, and hardly any lighting. No one had any small personal possessions or any change of clothing. The place was infested with sandflies, and the stagnant water of the moat bred a virulent kind of mosquito. We did not know when we should get supplies of fresh food or milk, and as there were only twelve cups and about twenty plates, distribution of what food we had was difficult. One could summon up courage to face these conditions oneself, but the presence of so many babies and children made the situation really serious. One baby had developed typhoid fever that morning, and they all had requirements which could not be met.

'Our numbers were swelling, for not everybody had managed to get to the rallying-posts. During the first night three survivors who had escaped into the police station were brought out of the city in Indian clothes. They told us of the infuriated crowds that had swept through the city on that terrible afternoon, drunk with their victory over unarmed men, and calling for "white blood". A Dutch merchant had hidden all day, and had come out at nightfall, disguised in a "burka", the all-enveloping white cloth used by purdah women. An English lady doctor had managed to conceal herself in her hospital while the crowd tried to find her, and she also had escaped in the evening. Two Indian ladies, schoolteachers, who had driven out of the city in a closed carriage, told us of the Sikh peasants who were pouring into the city with their iron-bound sticks. The booty from the National Bank had been carried out into the district as proof that the British rule was over, and all the riff-raff for miles round hurried in to be early on the spot if looting began again. The residents of the railway quarters came on to us from the railway station, in which they had taken refuge. They brought news of how the crowd had swept through the station, leaving behind them burning trucks and the hardly recognizable body of guard Robinson. Everything was done to stop false reports: under the conditions I have described, morale was of paramount importance. But the real truth was so often worse than anything rumour could invent that one realized the uses of censorship. It is not surprising that there was a certain amount of hysteria, but our people as a whole showed both courage and good sense.

'During the first three days every hour brought in some news from outside: of firing at Lahore, of murders at Kasur, of trains derailed and lines torn up, of telegraph wires cut and Government buildings and railway stations burnt; and we were very anxious about Europeans in the neighbourhood. The news was often vague, but with the breakdown in communications and our own experience we were left to imagine the worst, and the native population had some excuse for their belief that the British raj was over. The situation was so precarious, and troops for defensive purposes so scarce, that it was decided to evacuate the Alexandra School, just inside the Civil Lines, in which the Indian Christian School children had been collected until now. It might be supposed by English readers that these children would have been safe from their own countrymen, but on the day of the riots the crowd set fire to one school, with the girls inside, and it was only the timely arrival of a small band of police that saved them. We were told now to prepare to receive them, and when they arrived they brought our numbers up to about 400—a heavy strain on our resources, but they were grateful and worked splendidly.

'An office was established in the canteen hall, and all the civilian inhabitants of the Fort and their servants were registered. After a few days passes were issued for going out of the Fort, but this was not allowed without an armed escort, and everybody had to be back before sunset. The time at which the pass-holder was due to return was registered, so that if he or she failed to report at the office at the hour named a search party could be sent out immediately.

'The days were monotonous, and we had to keep very quiet for the sake of Miss Sherwood, who was lying between life and death'.

When day dawned on April 11th, the authorities at Amritsar, civil and military, knew not what to expect. The city was in the hands of a mob, all telephone and telegraph communications with the outside world were cut, and gangs of villagers, they learned, were tearing up railway tracks and derailing trains. The city of Lahore, the capital of the Province, was in the hands of the mob, Mr Kitchin told them. Inside Amritsar, a C.I.D. officer who came out in disguise, said gangs of rioters were marching about crying 'Murder the Europeans. This is the time that we should rise.'

'For all we knew, we were the only white men left in India', Commissioner Kitchin stated in 1924.

V

GENERAL DYER TAKES COMMAND

The code telegram General Dyer received at Jullundur at 4 p.m. on April 10th, saying that troops, guns and an aeroplane were needed urgently in Amritsar, was confirmed at 5.15 p.m. by a further telegram which told him that arson, looting and the murder of Europeans had taken place. The Divisional Commander at Lahore, General Sir William Beynon, requested him to dispatch a hundred British and a hundred Muslim troops to Amritsar at once. Dyer instructed his Brigade-Major, Captain Briggs, to send a telegram to Amritsar stating that help was on the way, a message which reached there by roundabout means. The relief force, consisting of a hundred British soldiers of the 1-25th London Regiment and two hundred Indians, a hundred more Indians than Dyer had been asked to send, left Jullundur in a special train at 1 a.m., reaching Amritsar at five o'clock on the morning of the 11th. Their Commander, Major F. A. S. Clarke, having handed them over to Major MacDonald, returned to Jullundur, where he reported to Dyer the existence 'of an unsatisfactory situation which the civil authorities had given up attempting to control'.

At 2 p.m. on the 11th an order came from the Divisional Commander for General Dyer to go himself to Amritsar, which was in his command, and to take such measures as he considered necessary to restore order. 'There is a big show coming', Dyer told his son, Captain Ivon Dyer, and before he left at 6 p.m. he ordered him to guard the bungalow where his mother and cousin Alice were living, telling him, 'You will sleep under a tree beside the verandah'.

April 11th passed peacefully in Amritsar. In the morning the Deputy Commissioner was told that large crowds were collecting and were proposing to accompany the funerals of those who had been killed the day before who, he learned, numbered between eight and eleven. Sending for two lawyers, Maqbool Mahmood and Mr Yasin, he dispatched them into the city to convey his order that not more than four people would be allowed to accompany each funeral cortege. In his testimony to the Congress Sub-Committee, Maqbool Mahmood had this to say:

'We then went to the city and explained the Deputy Commissioner's orders to the people. The people did not listen and insisted on a procession and said it was a religious function. We came back to the Deputy Commissioner with those whom the people sent with us. We explained the whole situation to him. His attitude was most offensive. He became very angry and was trembling. He shouted at us, "No more talking. We have seen our dead bodies charred. Our temper is changed." We expressed our sorrow for the murders. This drove him wild and he shouted out, "You are sorry now, you ought to have been sorry when you were attending those foolish meetings of yours, and you may be sorry before you leave." We simply said that we have never attended or addressed any foolish meetings and withdrew. Colonel Smith was present all the time at the station and suggested bombing of the city to quiet the mob.'

The funerals took place in the afternoon, large processions following them to the city gates and small parties only accompanying them to the burial and burning grounds. The people, says Dr Muhammad Abdullah Fauq, were very angry that they were not allowed to attend the funerals of 'the martyrs of their nation'. No excesses were committed and the funerals were finished by 4 p.m.

During the day Commissioner Kitchin, who remained in Amritsar in consultation with Mr Irving but who did not take over charge from him, received a number of reports from the outlying districts. The railway line between Amritsar and Lahore had been cut at Atari, a goods train derailed, the telegraph lines cut at Gurdaspur and Dhairiwal, he was told, and a number of Manjha Jats were collecting to enter and plunder the city. People were streaming out of the villages and there were the wildest rumours that the bazaars would be looted. The position at Lahore was difficult to ascertain because the only means of communication was by phonophone, which made hearing very hard. The information he received brought him to the conclusion, Mr Kitchin told the Hunter Committee, 'It was necessary to strike quickly and strike hard in order to save the rural people and above all to save the army from disaffection'. It was necessary, he considered, to inform the people that the authorities considered that a state of war had broken out, that they must settle down and that 'our patience was nearly exhausted'.

At noon the troops were marched into the city and a

proclamation was given to a number of lawyers for distribution, stating:

'The troops have orders to restore order in Amritsar and to use all force necessary. No gathering of persons nor processions of any sort will be allowed. All gatherings will be fired upon. Any persons leaving the city in groups of more than four will be fired on. Respectable persons should keep indoors.'

In addition, the Principal of the Khalsa College was asked to get his students to tell the people that the authorities considered that a state of war had broken out and they must settle down. All third class bookings to Amritsar from neighbouring stations were stopped in order to discourage innocent strangers from coming into so grave a situation. Orders were sent to village headmen in the district to keep watch and ward on the railways and magistrates were sent to several villages to organise local levees. In addition to these preventive measures, an armoured train was sent out to reconnoitre the position generally.

In the evening a large crowd, 20,000 strong, gathered at the house of Dr Bashir, the Secretary of the Satyagrahis, which caused so much noise that it awoke Dr Fauq, who went across the bazaar to see what was happening. Five hundred of the crowd, he learned, had been allowed inside the house, and their spokesman demanded that a resolution be passed to the effect that, if the Government agreed to take no steps about the disturbances on the 10th, the *hartal* would be brought to an end. Dr Bashir urged them to terminate the *hartal* and he warned them that no such assurance could be given. It was freely said in the city, states Dr Fauq, that while the Government ruled outside, the Hindus and Muslims ruled inside.

That night Commissioner Kitchin went to Lahore, where he had a conference with the Lieutenant Governor and the Officer Commanding troops, returning to Amritsar by motor car and seeing no signs of unrest on the road, which he found packed with traffic.

After a three-hour journey by road, General Dyer, who was accompanied by his staff officers, Captain Briggs and Captain Bostock, reached Amritsar at 9 p.m., finding, says his biographer, the railway station in a state of tumult, filled with fugitives clamouring for transport out of the city. 'Oh, Gentlemen, why are you here? Your place is to protect the ladies. You will report to me', Dyer told them.

Calling a conference in a railway coach, Dyer reviewed the situation with the Deputy Commissioner, his assistant and the Superintendent of Police. He was informed of the riots, murders, attacks on individuals and arson on the 10th and he was told particularly of the 'dastardly attack', as he later labelled it, on Miss Sherwood. He was informed that the authorities were not in possession of the city, which was in a state of lawlessness and open revolt, 'impenitently hostile', as Miles Irving described it. The situation was very critical, the Deputy Commissioner stated. There was a great danger from outside if the villagers rose. The situation had no parallel since the Mutiny, Mr Irving declared. The hotheads thought the Government was failing. An influx of country people threatened to swell the ranks of the mob, and it was said that a *Danda Fauj*, a 'bludgeon army', was to be formed which would drive out the British by 'slaps alone'. Arrangements had been made to arm it and large consignments of sticks were on the way.

In the evidence he gave to the Hunter Committee General Dyer stated that he was asked by the civil authorities to take control. Miles Irving said he could not deal with the situation, that it was beyond civil control and that 'I should take matters in hand', Dyer stated. He understood the position to be that civil law was at an end and that military law would have to take its place for the time being. It was necessary for him to act without the actual declaration of martial law; the position relieving him of the necessity of consulting the civil authority of the district.

According to Mr Ian Colvin, General Dyer's biographer, at this time 'Mr Miles Irving looked like a man broken by fatigue, anxiety and the weight of responsibility too heavy for his shoulders', and he tells us that 'the easy confidence and manifest strength of the General must have been very reassuring to this harassed individual, who freely handed over a situation altogether beyond his control'. 'To await events was not the General's way', declares Mr Colvin and he goes on to say, 'How was he to fight the rebels, how was he to bring them to decisive action in the narrow streets and winding lanes of Amritsar? It was a problem, as he afterwards explained to Mrs Dyer, which seemed to him, with his little force, insoluble, unless, indeed, he could get them somehow in the open. And that seemed too much to hope for.'

The troops at General Dyer's disposal consisted of 475 British and 710 Indian soldiers, composed as follows: the original garrison consisting of 184 officers and men of the Somerset Light Infantry and forty-one men of the 12th Ammunition Column, R.A.; the 277 Gurkhas detrained at Amritsar on the 10th; the 130 men of the 2-6th Battalion of the Royal Sussex Regiment (who were sent back to Lahore on the 13th), thirteen men manning the two armoured cars equipped with machine guns and 181 men of the 1-124th Baluchis, who had arrived from Lahore during the night of the 10th; and the force sent from Jullundur on the 11th, consisting of 107 men of the 1-25th London Regiment, twenty-one men of the 54th Sikhs, 101 men of the 59th Rifles and 130 men of the 2-151st Infantry.

Before him stood a city filled with 160,000 people in open rebellion, Dyer believed, and around him lay country seething with discontent. Riots and disturbances had occurred, he knew, in Lahore and in other cities, and he believed himself almost completely isolated with his small force. 'I thought they were trying to isolate me and my forces', he told the Hunter Committee and he said, 'Everything pointed to the fact that there was a widespread movement, and that it was not confined to Amritsar alone. I looked upon these men as rebels who were trying to isolate my forces and cut me off from other supplies.'

That night, at 12.30 a.m., General Dyer marched with a small force to the Kotwali, seeing no mob but finding the fires still burning in several looted buildings. He brought Inspector Ashraf Khan out in order to ascertain from him the names of the ringleaders of the riot. He then proceeded to reorganize his forces, reducing the pickets in order to build up a larger striking force.

Next morning, after the city had been surveyed by an aeroplane sent from Lahore, the pilot of which reported that all was quiet, Dyer marched through Amritsar with 125 British troops and 310 Indian soldiers and two armoured cars, finding insolent crowds, who shouted slogans and spat on the ground, assembled at the Sultanwind Gate, which he had some difficulty in dispersing. He considered the advisability of opening fire, but he thought it would not be quite right to take such a drastic measure until he had issued a proclamation personally, he told the Hunter Committee.

This he issued through the police, stating:

'The inhabitants of Amritsar are hereby warned that if they will cause damage to any property or will commit any acts of violence in the environments of Amritsar, it will be taken for granted that such acts have been committed in Amritsar City itself and the offenders will be punished according to military law. All meetings and gatherings are hereby prohibited and will be dispersed at once under military law.'

The police, acting under military protection, made twelve arrests of ringleaders of the mob, and after they had been brought out of the city, Dyer heard that a meeting had been held at the Hindu Sabha High School demanding their release.

On his return to Headquarters in the Ram Bagh, Dyer was told that a report had come that the Fort at Lahore had been taken, that the Indian troops had mutinied and that the Lieutenant-Governor had been killed. Disturbing rumours, the impact of which was not lessened by the request from Lahore that Dyer should send back some of his British troops, to which Commissioner Kitchin replied, 'I am anxious not to reduce the British force until we know that the Indian troops are sound', and a message was sent to Lahore stating, 'Baluchis on guard are showing some sign of insubordination', a suggestion of disloyalty which General Dyer subsequently denied.

Messages and reports informed Dyer of the situation. A report received by aeroplane stated that Lahore was quiet, but that the station at Kasur had been wrecked and two Europeans murdered. The armoured train sent out on the 11th reported that the stations beyond Kasur were quiet. All telegraph wires between Amritsar and Lahore were cut, stated the Telegraph Master. Near at hand the news was more disturbing. The country people living near Amritsar were flooding into the city, Dyer was told, bringing with them ox carts and donkeys to carry away the loot they hoped to get. That night a small force was sent to the village of Tarn Taran where trouble had been reported, but through a misunderstanding it returned to Amritsar and, on its departure, a crowd tried to loot the Treasury, being deterred by an Inspector of Police with a small force who putting on a bold front drove the crowd away.

On Sunday morning, April 13th, General Dyer, accompanied by the Deputy Commissioner and the Superintendent of Police, set out from the Ram Bagh to march through Amritsar in order to make a proclamation, which was read at nineteen prominent places at beat of drum. The procession was led by Inspector Ashraf Khan, riding a white horse, who was followed by a bamboo cart in which sat the drummer and Malik Fateh Khan, whom Mr Irving describes as 'a sort of unofficial public orator, a man who had great natural charm of oratory, much in demand on ceremonial occasions'. The proclamation was read twice in Urdu at each place and it was explained twice in Punjabee, the language of the common people, of whom some 500 collected to hear each reading. The crowds were laughing and 'not behaving very well', according to Dyer. Malik Fateh Khan told the Hunter Committee that the people 'all jeered' and Sub-Inspector Obaidullah testified he heard people say, 'We will hold a meeting; let us be fired on'. Dyer was told that people were saying, 'This is all bluff; he won't fire'. 'Let them do what they will; we will hold a meeting', Dr Fauq heard people shouting near the Kotwali.

Two separate proclamations were read. The first stated:

'The inhabitants of Amritsar are warned by means of this proclamation that if they damage any property or commit any act of violence in the neighbourhood of Amritsar, such acts will be considered to have been instigated from the city of Amritsar, and we shall arrange to punish the inhabitants of Amritsar in accordance with the military law. All meetings and assemblies are prohibited by this proclamation, and we shall act in accordance with the military law in order to disperse all such assemblies forthwith.'

The second ordered:

1. 'It is hereby notified that no inhabitant of Amritsar is permitted to go out of the city in his own or in a hired conveyance or on foot without obtaining a pass from the undermentioned officers' (listing nine).
2. 'No inhabitant of the city is permitted to go out of his house after 8 p.m. Persons going out into the street after 8 p.m. will be liable to be shot.'
3. 'No procession is permitted at any time in the bazaars or in any part of the city or at any place outside the city. Any such procession or gathering will be considered illegal, and will be dealt with accordingly, and, if necessary, will be dispersed by means of arms.'

Both proclamations were signed by Brigadier General R. E. Dyer, Commander, 45 Brigade.

At the meeting of the Hunter Committee, at which he gave evidence, Dyer was asked the significance of the qualification 'if necessary'. He replied, 'It may not always be necessary'. He said he was quite justified, if he told the people to disperse and they refused to do so, in dispersing them by force of arms because 'they had defied my authority and it would not be necessary in my opinion to say to them any more'.

While the column was marching round the city making the proclamation, four Indians paraded the streets, one beating an empty kerosene tin and another announcing that a meeting would be held that afternoon. At 12.40 p.m. General Dyer was told that a meeting in the Jallianwala Bagh was planned for that afternoon. As it was getting too hot for his troops, he ordered the column to return to the Ram Bagh.

At 4 p.m. Superintendent Rehill came to inform Dyer that Mr Lewis, the manager of the Crown Cinema, had come out of the city in disguise to report that the meeting was being held. Questioned by the Hunter Committee as to why he made no attempt to prevent it being held, General Dyer answered, 'I went there as soon as I could. I had to think the matter out, I had to organize my forces and make up my mind as to where I might put my pickets. I thought I had done enough to make the crowd not meet. If they were going to meet, I had to consider the military situation and make up my mind what to do, which took me a certain amount of time.'

On receiving Mr. Lewis's report, Dyer decided to proceed to the Jallianwala Bagh which was situated in the heart of the city, about a mile and a half from the Ram Bagh. The opportunity had come for him to strike the decisive blow, suggests his biographer who puts the position General Dyer faced thus:

'He could not remain on the defensive. His forces were not only small; part of them was wanted elsewhere, and the rebellion was spreading. On the 10th the mob had struck a blow that was reverberating over India. It had given heart to their cause. They had tasted blood, they had not been punished, they began to feel themselves masters of the situation. Therefore, with a wasting force, he opposed a growing force. His best hope lay in immediate action.

'So much was clear. But how to strike? In the narrow streets, among the high houses and mazy lanes and courtyards of the city the rebels had the advantage of position. They could harass him and avoid his blow. Street fighting he knew to be a bloody, perilous, inconclusive business, in which, besides, the innocent

GENERAL DYER TAKES COMMAND

were likely to suffer more than the guilty. Moreover, if the rebels chose their ground cunningly, and made their stand in the neighbourhood of the Golden Temple, there was the added risk of kindling the fanaticism of the Sikhs. Thus he was in this desperate situation; he could not wait, and he could not fight.

'But this unexpected gift of fortune, this unhoped for defiance, this concentration of the rebels in an open space—it gave him such an opportunity as he could not have devised. It separated the guilty from the innocent, it placed them where he would have wished them to be—within reach of his sword. The enemy had committed such another mistake as prompted Cromwell to explain at Dunbar, "the Lord hath delivered them into my hands".'

Dyer reviewed his forces. Of his 407 British and 739 Indian troops, 389 British and 382 Indian were already allocated to various duties:

British:	Station pickets	37
	Bridge guards	11
	Detachment at Tarn Taran	22
	Armoured trains	43
	Fort Gobina Garh	86
	Cantonment	190
Indian:	Detachment at Tarn Taran	34
	Detachment at Dharival	26
	Detachment at Atari	40
	Train escorts	80
	Line repair escorts	10
	Construction train	10
	Blockhouse on railway	40
	Pickets	132
	Kotwali in city	50

He needed to leave a strong guard at his headquarters, and when this had been allocated, he set out accompanied by 200 men, a hundred of whom were dropped off as pickets as the column proceeded through the city. When he turned into the bazaar from which the Jallianwala Bagh led, General Dyer had with him ninety Indian troops, fifty of them armed with rifles and forty with knives, and the men manning the two armoured cars. In one military car sat General Dyer and Captain Briggs, in another Mr Rehill and Mr Plomer. The Sepoys marched in front and behind.

C.I.D. Inspector Jowahal Lal was already in the Jallianwala Bagh, where his 'plain clothes' saved him from recognition by the crowd, whom he heard exclaiming, 'What do we care for military orders? What can the military do?' Pratap Singh was one of the crowd. Five months later he told the Congress Sub-Committee:

'I heard no proclamation at all on April 13th, declaring Martial Law or prohibiting public meetings. Nor did any such proclamation reach my Bazaar on that day. I reached the Jallianwala Bagh about 4 p.m. with my son, Kirpa Singh, nine years old. I went to hear Babu Kanhya Lal's lecture, because that was advertised in our Bazaar. About half an hour after my arrival, the noise of an aeroplane was heard. I was about a dozen paces distant on the side of the platform where the entrance was. Hans Raj spoke. He had put up the picture of Dr Kitchlew and said that his portrait would preside. He said that men were wrongfully shot on the 10th, because they were going at that time to make a complaint to the Deputy Commissioner. He also said that a resolution should be passed asking for the repeal of the Rowlatt Act. Gopinath then read a poem about the faryad of the people not being heard. There was nothing at all in what I heard which was against the Government.'

Then he saw the soldiers rushing into the Bagh.

The Amritsar *War Diary* for April 13, 1919, states that the crowd was dispersed by fire and it records that 1,650 rounds were fired, the casualties being estimated at from 200 to 300. The city was 'absolutely quiet and not a soul to be seen' that night when General Dyer marched through Amritsar to see if his orders had been obeyed.

VI

'THE DECISIVE FACTOR'

The first news of the firing in the Jallianwala Bagh reached Lahore at 11.15 p.m. in a garbled message received by the Deputy Inspector-General of Police, Mr Farquhar, who telephoned it to Mr Thompson, the Chief Secretary, which stated that a prohibited meeting had been dispersed and there were rumours of heavy casualties. More complete information arrived at 3 a.m. on the 14th, when Mr Waythen, Principal of the Sikh Khalsa College in Amritsar, and Mr Jacob of the Indian Civil Service brought a letter from the Deputy Commissioner written at 1 a.m. Sir Michael O'Dwyer and Mr Kitchin, the Commissioner, were roused and they read the letter together. Mr Miles Irving said that a proclamation had been read in the city prohibiting public meetings. He went on:

'A meeting had been advertised for 4.30 that day, and the General said he would attend it with 100 men. I did not think that the meeting would be held, or if held would disperse, so I asked the General to excuse me, as I wanted to go to the Fort.

'I learn that the Military found a large meeting of some five thousand men, and opened fire without warning, killing about two hundred. Firing went on for about ten minutes.

'I went through the city at night with the General, and all was absolutely still.

'I much regret that I was not present, but when out previously with the Military the greatest forebearance had been used in making the people disperse. I had absolutely no idea of the action taken.'

Without waiting for further information, Sir Michael O'Dwyer at once sent a wireless message to Simla, stating:

'At Amritsar yesterday Brig.-General Dyer and Deputy Commissioner read proclamation in city forbidding all public meetings. Proclamation proclaimed by beat of drum and read and explained at several places in city. In spite of this, meeting attended by 6,000 was held at 4.30 contrary to Deputy Commissioner's expectation. Troops present under command of General Dyer fired, killing about 200. Deputy Commissioner not present. Military report not yet received. City quiet at night but political effect on Manjha (the Sikh tract around Lahore and Amritsar) and troops uncertain. In view of possibilities General Officer Commanding is arranging to draft into Lahore more troops, British and Indian.'

The Lieutenant-Governor of the Punjab expressed no opinion about General Dyer's action, and he was told by the messengers, incorrectly, that Dyer had used only British troops as the Indian troops had refused to fire, and that no civil officer had been with him. O'Dwyer sent Commissioner Kitchin back to Amritsar.

During the morning of the 14th, General Sir William Beynon received a despatch from Dyer reporting his operations from April 11th, in which he stated the inhabitants of Amritsar had been warned, if they held meetings, they would be fired on. Coming to the events of the 13th, he reported:

'I entered the Jallianwala Bagh by a very narrow lane which necessitated my leaving my armoured cars behind.

'On entering I saw a dense crowd estimated at about 5,000, a man on a raised platform addressing the audience and making gesticulations with his hands.

'I realized my force was small and to hesitate might induce attack. I immediately opened fire and dispersed the crowd.

'I estimate that between 200 and 300 of the crowd were killed. My party fired 1,650 rounds.'

Beynon telephoned O'Dwyer, giving him the substance of Dyer's report and telling him that Dyer's action had crushed the rebellion at Amritsar at its heart. Not only in Amritsar, O'Dwyer replied. As the news of the firing in the Jallianwala Bagh got around, he said, it would prevent its spreading elsewhere. Beynon told O'Dwyer he was sending a message to General Dyer stating, 'Your Action Correct'. Could he add 'Lieutenant-Governor Approves?' enquired the Divisional Commander. O'Dwyer, who was fully occupied by reports of disturbances which were pouring in, says in his book *India As I knew It* he made no note of the telephone conversation except that he was struck by the reassuring news that Indian and Gurkha troops had been used and that General Dyer had been accompanied by the Superintendent of Police. He had at first, he says, some hesitation in complying with Beynon's request as Dyer's action was a military one, but 'on further reflection I thought it advisable to endorse General Beynon's approval', he says. The time was not one for disputing the necessity for military action, he told the Hunter Committee, and he explained, 'I approved of General Dyer's action in dispersing by force the rebellious gathering and thus preventing further rebellious acts. It was not for me to say he had gone too far when I was told by his superior officer that he fully approved of General Dyer's action.'

The substance of Dyer's report was transmitted to Simla by wireless and, we learn from Captain L. V. S. Blacker of the Guides (*On Secret Patrol In High Asia*) that it was picked up by the Bolsheviks, who were trying to negotiate an anti-British alliance with the Amir of Afganistan, for he says, 'The Soviet-Afgan defeat in the Jallianwala Bagh at Amritsar, on the Khyber line, had rather disgusted our sporting cousins of Kabul and Kandahar'.

The Government of India passed on Dyer's report to London and on April 18th the India Office issued a statement about the Punjab disturbances which said:

'At Amritsar April 13th the mob defied the proclamation forbidding public meetings. Firing ensued and 200 casualties occurred.'

No one in London, apparently, gave the matter a second thought. Six months were to elapse before Amritsar became news in England and the name of the Jallianwala Bagh a household word.

The story of how the news of the Jallianwala Bagh firing was brought to Lahore and transmitted to London has carried us ahead of events. On the 13th, after consulting with General Beynon and the Chief Justice, Sir Henry Rattigan, Sir Michael O'Dwyer sent this message to the Government of India by wireless:

'Railway stations between Kasur and Amritsar looted. British soldier killed and two British officers injured at Kasur. Bands of rebels reported on move. Kasur and Tarn Taran Treasuries attacked. State of open rebellion exists in parts of districts of Lahore and Amritsar. Lieutenant Governor, with concurrence of General Officer Commanding 16th Division and Chief Justice High Court, requests Governor General in Council to suspend functions of ordinary criminal courts in Amritsar and Lahore districts, to establish martial law therein and to direct trial of

F

offenders under Section 2 of Regulation X of 1804. Section 4 (allowing trial by ordinary courts instead of by courts martial where the latter procedure is not indisputably necessary) should be borne in mind. Situation critical. Moveable column starts on march from Ferozepore to Amritsar through worst tract with guns tomorrow morning.'

The Government of India at once sanctioned the imposition of martial law in the Punjab, stating that, 'The Governor General is satisfied that a state of open rebellion against the authority of the government exists in certain parts of the Province of the Punjab', but, due to the difficulties of communication, their order was not received by Sir Michael O'Dwyer until the 14th, the day described by him as 'the high watermark of the rebellion'. These powers were, he says, a most potent weapon in combating the disorders. Martial law had not been used in India since the Mutiny and he explains that 'its unexpected production had immediate and most salutary results'. Foreseeing, however, the difficulties likely to arise from the exercise of these novel powers by inexperienced officers he says he desired from the start to keep the administration of martial law under civilian control. But when he informed the Government of India of his intention, he received an emphatic veto. Martial law powers were vested in the General Officer Commanding Troops, he was told, and 'he only can exercise those powers'. There was no power for the Lieutenant Governor to take the line he proposed. Thus, in effect, O'Dwyer observes, the civil government had to stand aside. It could give advice but it rested with the military authorities to accept or reject it. The soldiers, O'Dwyer points out, had to consider the situation from the military standpoint, a matter upon which he dwells, he says in his memoirs, due to the issues raised in the libel action he brought subsequently against an Indian who was in 1919 a member of the government.

The martial law ordinance suspended the functions of the ordinary criminal courts and established special commissioners to try offences arising from the disturbances, and it was back dated to March 30th. At Sir Michael O'Dwyer's suggestion, death as the only penalty which could be imposed upon conviction for rebellion, for waging war against the King Emperor, was mitigated by the alternative punishments of transportation and rigorous imprisonment.

The Government of India passed on the 14th, says Sir Michael

O'Dwyer, a special Resolution asserting 'in the clearest possible manner', their intention to prevent by all means, however drastic, any recurrence of the excesses that had occurred, and which declared that the Governor-General 'will not hesitate to employ the ample resources at its disposal to suppress organized outrage, rioting, or concerted opposition to the maintenance of law and order', and the Resolution stated, 'To those servants of Government who are charged with the onerous responsibility of suppressing excesses against public peace and tranquility, the Governor-General in Council extends the fullest assurance of countenance and support'. 'Brave words', says O'Dwyer, which were quickly forgotten when the crisis which inspired them had passed.

O'Dwyer stated in 1924 that he was told on April 12th on the telephone by an official of the Home Department at Simla that, if troops had to fire, they should make an example.

The situation on April 14th, as O'Dwyer saw it, was still menacing. Looting, arson and murder had occurred in Lahore, Kasur and Amritsar. Rail lines and telegraph wires had been cut all over the province. Trains had been derailed and minor disturbances had occurred in many small towns and villages. Order had been restored, for the moment, in the chief cities. April 14th brought news of a major outbreak, this time at Gujranwala, and several smaller ones in half-a-dozen places, which had broken out before the salutary news from Amritsar had time to take effect. Railway strikes were reported from several important junctions, all part, Sir Michael O'Dwyer considered, of a concerted movement, a most serious development for the paralysis of transport would make it impossible to move troops to crush the rebellion, which he believed to be still rapidly spreading.

'The Gujranwala disturbance came on us rather as a shock', says O'Dwyer, and it was inspired, he believed, by the news of the disorders in Amritsar and Lahore. No trouble occurred at Gujranwala, a town of 25,000 inhabitants thirty-seven miles from Lahore, between April 6th to 13th, but at 7 a.m. on the 14th the police received a report that the body of a dead calf was hanging on the bridge by the railway station. As such an exhibition was likely to foment bad blood between Hindus and Muslims, it was removed but not before news of its presence had circulated. Shops were closed and crowds collected at the station, stopping and stoning a train which arrived from Lahore. A mob set the bridge on fire, destroyed the telegraph wires for a hundred yards and did considerable damage at the station before Police Superintendent Heron arrived with a posse of armed police at 11 a.m. He was greeted with cries of 'Kill him, kill him'. He gave the order to fire, himself firing his revolver, two or three of the mob being wounded, an action approved by the Hunter Committee. Driven from the railway station the mob streamed back into the town, setting fire to the Post Office, the Deputy Commissioner, an Indian, failing to give the police an order to fire, a dereliction of duty which the Hunter Committee found was open to criticism. All Europeans were hurriedly collected and taken to the Treasury. There were no troops in the town. Messages requesting help were sent to Lahore, where they were communicated to Sir Michael O'Dwyer about 1 p.m.

No troops were available nearer than Rawalpindi, 200 miles away, he was told, and they could not reach Gujranwala before evening. 'The position seemed somewhat hopeless', observes O'Dwyer. A dangerous situation existed in Gujranwala. An inexperienced Indian civil officer was in charge, for the Deputy Commissioner, Colonel O'Brien, had recently been transferred. He was still in Lahore, O'Dwyer learned, and by 1.30 p.m. Colonel O'Brien was on his way back to Gujranwala, accompanied by a small escort. O'Dwyer conferred with General Beynon. There were no troops to send. What about aeroplanes? he enquired. The question of using aeroplanes in civil disturbances had already been discussed, he says, and it had been agreed that they should not bomb inhabited areas as they might injure innocent people, but they could fly low and use machine guns under the same conditions as troops would use rifles. Colonel Minchin, in command of the Air Force, was called in and it was agreed to send three planes to Gujranwala under these conditions.

One of these planes was flown by Captain D. H. M. Carberry, M.C., D.F.C., and before taking off he was told 'that the native city was not to be bombed unless necessary and crowds were to be bombed only if in the open'. Flying at low level he saw a crowd of about 150 people outside the village of Dhulla, two miles northwest of Gujranwala. He dropped three bombs; one failed to explode and two fell near the party, scattering it. Three people were seen to drop and it was learned afterwards that a woman and a boy were killed and two men slightly wounded. As the people ran for cover, Captain Carberry fired fifty rounds from his machine gun to ensure that they dispersed effectively.

Continuing his flight, he spotted a group of about fifty people outside the village of Gharjakh, one mile to the southwest of Gujranwala. He dropped two bombs, one exploding. The crowd ran into the village, Captain Carberry firing twenty-five rounds without visible effect. Turning towards Gujranwala, he saw a party of about 200 people assembled in a field near a large red building, which was in fact the Khalsa High School. He dropped one bomb which burst in the courtyard, apparently wounding several people, and he fired thirty rounds at a party which took refuge in a house, three boys being hit and wounded. He then carried on over the town, dropping various bombs, their location being uncertain and their number inexact, two of which burst near the railway level crossing near the station, killing six and wounding a dozen people. He fired 100 to 150 rounds upon parties who appeared to be proceeding from the station towards the civil lines. Captain Carberry then returned to Lahore, landing at 3.50 p.m. Of the other two planes dispatched, one took no action, the other firing twenty-five rounds at a crowd near the level crossing. One of their pilots, Lieutenant Kirby, on his return journey was forced to land in a field near Wazirbad. Rioters, he reported, approached his machine, proposing to burn it but he managed to restart his engine and fly away.

At 8.30 p.m. Captain Harrison arrived by train with a platoon of Durham Light Infantry and a railway track repair gang. At Colonel O'Brien's request another aeroplane was sent over Gujranwala next day to assist him, by overawing the people, to restore order. Its pilot, Lieutenant Dodkins, dropped one bomb, which blew in the side of a house and he fired his machine gun on a crowd which scattered, inflicting, as far as is known, no casualties. Order was restored in the town in which eleven people had been killed and twenty-seven wounded.

The Hunter Committee, considering the decision to use aeroplanes at Gujranwala, found it justified with the object of saving the lives of the threatened Europeans, especially as there was no certainty of the troops reaching the town in time. It observed that in the attacks on villages, the element of immediate and manifest urgency was lacking. While it did not impute blame on the officer for his decision taken in the air and at the moment, the Committee did not feel certain that the machine gunning of villagers was necessary. Captain Carberry's decision to use bombs was just, but the orders he was given were defective. The Committee upheld his action in dropping bombs in the city for 'these bombs appeared to have fallen in the midst of rioters caught in the act of rioting and fully minded to continue'. The bombs were, therefore, 'justified and invaluable' in restoring order. The minority of the Indian members of the Committee condemned Captain Carberry's action.

Disturbances occurred also in several places in the Gujranwala district, inhabited, Sir Michael O'Dwyer observes, by a million people and which was controlled only by a few British officers without troops. The news of the riots in Gujranwala, he says, spread along the railway line which ran northwest to the Indus and the North West Frontier and west to Lyallpur, the richest agricultural province of India. These outbreaks he attributed to the work of local agitators, lawyers of the Congress Party, who were in touch with the ringleaders of revolt at Amritsar. A determined attempt was made, he declared, to work up the Sikh colonists by false rumours that the Sikh Temple at Amritsar had been bombed and Sikh girls had been outraged by British soldiers. The danger of a possible rising of the excitable and virile Sikhs was, he believed, more real than that from the rabble in the towns. Measures taken locally by British officials, he says, saved the situation until troops arrived in the district on April 17th. A menacing situation in Gurdaspur, in which there was a scattered community of European and American missionaries, was alleviated by the prompt action of General Dyer, who detached troops from Amritsar to the danger spot. At Nizamabad, a crowd collected outside the empty house of a missionary, Mr Graham Bailey, who had been evacuated with his family. When the ringleaders suggested that the house be burned, some members of the mob, according to the Hunter Committee, 'demurred on the ground that he was an Irishman and therefore against the government', but despite this remarkable protest, the house was burned down. Mobs at Hafizabad, Dhaban and Sangla attacked individuals, and trains were derailed and telegraph wires cut.

The situation on April 16th, as Sir Michael O'Dwyer saw it, was that in twenty-nine districts of the Punjab, having a population of between three and four million, more than half of them without troops, things were still dangerous. In a wireless message to Simla he stated that the rural population was joining in the looting of trains and that persistent attempts were being made to seduce troops, but they had proved staunch everywhere 'so far', and he gave the reassuring information that there was nothing to suggest that the Sikhs were prominent in the rebellion.

No disorders and no firing occurred after April 16th. The riots petered out as the news of the firing in the Jallianwala Bagh spread. Everywhere, says Mr Miles Irving, the cry was, 'The Sahibs are shooting'. In his written statement prepared for the Hunter Committee, Commissioner Kitchin says, 'All independent opinion is united that the blow struck on April 13th saved the Central Punjab from anarchy, loot and murder'. Six months later, Sir Michael O'Dwyer told the Hunter Committee:

'Speaking with perhaps a more intimate knowledge of the then situation than anyone else, I have no hesitation in saying that General Dyer's action that day was the decisive factor in crushing the rebellion, the seriousness of which is only now being realized.'

VII

THE CRAWLING ORDER

The receipt of his superior officers' approval of the action he had taken in the Jallianwala Bagh must have given General Dyer considerable satisfaction, especially as it was endorsed by the Lieutenant-Governor of the Punjab. The message 'Your action correct. Lieutenant-Governor approves' was brought to Dyer at the Court House in the Civil Lines, to where he had moved his headquarters on the morning of the 14th. A few hours before he had killed between two and three hundred natives, he believed. He fired entirely on his own responsibility and without taking advice. In his report he had justified himself by implying that the meeting had gathered in violation of his proclamation, and because his force was a small one, and 'to hesitate might incite attack'.

Justified and correct as Dyer thought his action, he would have been a strange man indeed if no niggling doubts had assailed him about his conduct and the views his superiors might take of it. He had acted ruthlessly; in his own opinion, fearlessly and justifiably. The mob had disobeyed his orders. He had fired, done his duty, horrible though it was. He had brought the rioters out into the open and destroyed them. He had saved Amritsar, the Punjab and all India. But would those to whom he was responsible see it that way? Now support, double-barrelled approval, had come from his military and political superiors. The tiny strands of doubt faded; his fears dissolved. The first stage of the process of thought by which General Dyer came to see himself as the Hero of the Hour was established; a self-created pedestal which as time went on became to him firmer and loftier. A pedestal like a musical stool, which rose higher and higher as Dyer plunged himself deeper and deeper into the miasma of self-delusion.

That morning, at eight o'clock, when Commissioner Kitchin came from Lahore, Dyer enquired of him, 'What will be the effect of the shooting?' and he declared, 'I have done my duty. It was a horrible duty. I haven't slept all night, but it was the right thing to do.' Kitchin's answer must have reassured him, 'the trouble will be over', and he told Dyer that Sir Michael

O'Dwyer was sorry the shooting had happened and he had sent him to take care that there should be no more firing if it could possibly be helped. The Deputy Commissioner must have said much the same, for Miles Irving told the Hunter Committee that the news of the 13th, as it spread, 'ended all dangers of further disturbances in the district'. 'It was taken far and wide', he said, 'as an assurance that the hand of the Government was not, as it was thought, paralyzed and all who were waiting on events hastened to declare for constituted authority.'

The events of the 14th must have further reassured Dyer. The situation in Amritsar returned to normal with amazing rapidity, so much so that he was able to tell the Hunter Committee, 'the city was soon a pattern of law and order'. A deputation of traders came to him, asking to be allowed to open their shops, and the leading citizens and municipal councillors assembled to express their 'admiration for my firm action' which they told him 'had saved Amritsar and other cities in the Punjab from complete plunder and bloodshed'. When Mr Kitchin toured the city that day he found, he said, 'smiling faces everywhere'.

Everyone, it seemed, was pleased with him, Dyer must have thought. He issued a proclamation permitting the burial of the dead and he made an order drafting the court pleaders and barristers of the city to act as special constables to maintain order, men who, with a few exceptions, did what was required of them, he said.

According to Girdhari Lal, the local businessman who, we recall, watched the firing in the Jallianwala Bagh through binoculars, both Dyer and Mr Kitchin made speeches to people assembled at the Kotwali. Commissioner Kitchin is alleged to have said:

'You people want peace or war? We are prepared in every way. The Government is all-powerful. Sarkar (the Government) has conquered Germany, and is capable of doing everything. The General will give orders today. The city is in his possession. I can do nothing. You will have to obey orders.'

Dyer also spoke, alleges Girdhari Lal:

'You people know well that I am a soldier and a military man. You want war or peace? And if you wish for war, the Government is prepared for war. And if you want peace, then obey my orders. and open all your shops, else I will shoot. For me the battlefield of France or Amritsar is the same. I am a military man, and will go straight, neither shall I move to the right nor to the left. Speak up, if you want war. In case there is to be peace, my order is to open all shops at once. You people talk against the Government, and persons educated in Germany and Bengal talk sedition. I shall uproot these all. Obey orders. I do not wish to hear anything else. I have served in the military for over thirty years. I understand the Indian Sepoy and Sikh people very well. You will have to observe peace, otherwise the shops will be opened perforce with rifles. You all must inform me of the badmashes. I will shoot them. Obey my orders and open shops and speak up if you want war.'

The whole of his speech was in the same strain, declares Girdhari Lal, who says Dyer was followed by Mr Miles Irving, the Deputy Commissioner, who spoke in a very bitter tone and said:

'You have heard the order of the General. The whole city is in his charge. His order is to open shops. Desirable for you to obey. If anyone has any trouble, say so, I shall listen. You have committed a bad act in killing the English. Their revenge will be taken from you and from your children. You people must open shops at once. The Government is very angry with you. You cannot fight the Government. I shall severely punish anyone who will talk against the Government.'

The truth or otherwise of these reported remarks must be left to the opinion of the individual reader, it being observed only that they would have been strange words for an Indian to have invented, especially the statement that revenge would be taken 'from you and your children', words which smack of knowledge of the New Testament.

The only disquieting views received by General Dyer on the 14th was the information brought to him by Mr MacDonald, the Inspector-General of Police who had come with Mr Kitchin from Lahore, that he had heard it was proposed to hold a meeting at the Golden Temple, the Sikh shrine, with the intention of inciting General Dyer's fire, with the result that the bullets would hit the Temple, whereupon the whole Sikh community would be up in arms as one man, which would lead to a mutiny of Sikh soldiers. There were persistent rumours, too, Dyer was told, that British soldiers had raped a party of Sikh girls at the railway station. He sent for the manager of the Golden Temple and the leader of the Sikh community, telling them that he would protect and not harm the Temple and asking them to refute these rumours. The story about the girls, he explained, arose from their male escorts being searched because they carried their traditional daggers, the *Kirpan*. The girls had not been molested, and he asked these officers to assist him in keeping the Sikhs out of the rebellion. General Dyer thus earned not only the confidence but the love and gratitude of the Sikhs, declares his biographer, who relates that when he returned to Amritsar at the end of April, General Dyer and his Brigade-Major, Captain Briggs, were summoned to the Golden Temple, where they found themselves in the presence of the chief priests and the leaders of the sect.

'Sahib', they said, 'you must become a Sikh even as Nikalseyn Sahib (General Nicholson of Mutiny fame) became a Sikh.'

The General thanked them for the honour, but he objected that he could not as a British officer let his hair grow long.

Arur Singh laughed. 'We will let you off the long hair', he said.

General Dyer offered another objection, 'But I cannot give up smoking'.

'That you must do', said Arur Singh.

'No,' said the General, 'I am very sorry, but I cannot give up smoking.'

The priest conceded, 'We will let you give it up gradually'.

'That I promise to,' said the General, 'at the rate of one cigarette a year.'

Mr Ian Colvin continues his charming little story:

'The Sikhs, chuckling, proceeded with the initiation. General Dyer and Captain Briggs were invested with the five *Kakas*, the sacred emblems of that war-like brotherhood, and so became Sikhs. Moreover, a shrine was built to General Dyer at their holy place, Guru Sat Sultani, and when a few days afterwards came the news that the Afghans were making war on India, the Sikh leaders offered the General 10,000 men to fight for the British Raj if only he would consent to command them. General Dyer reported this offer, but it was refused, and a magnificent impulse of loyalty was allowed to fade away.'

Martial law was proclaimed in Amritsar on April 15th, and General Dyer appointed its Administrator, thus recognizing the *de facto* military control of the city which had existed since the night of the 10th. 'The history of the rising henceforth', states Mr Miles Irving, 'is merely the record of progress in bringing offenders to justice and in dispelling the wild rumours that were in constant circulation and in quieting the minds of the people.'

General Dyer took measures to restore confidence. Villages in the district were patrolled 'to show', in Dyer's words, 'that the Sarkar was still strong and had soldiers and guns', and he made a tour himself, talking to the country people, advising them to settle down and warning them of the acts which would bring them within the scope of martial law. The situation had been threatening but since the 13th it was 'very much more satisfactory' he was told by the magistrate at Gurdaspur. False rumours needed to be refuted, he knew, and on April 18th he caused a proclamation to be issued in the name of the Deputy Commissioner. This stated:

'Ignorant and wicked people have circulated false rumours, and it is the intention of the Government that real facts be known. It is necessary for the help of Government that no such false rumours should get circulated. It is desirable that information regarding all such ridiculous news be at once communicated to the Deputy Commissioner so that he may be able to contradict false news and promulgate the correct news.

'The real facts regarding the incident that took place on Sunday in the city of Amritsar are as follows:

'The General Sahib had issued a proclamation that no gathering should assemble without his permission, no meeting be held and no procession take place. The General Sahib and myself went in person to the city and warned the residents of the city by beat of drum that, in case any meeting was held it would, if necessary be dispersed by means of bullets. Disregarding this order of the General Sahib, some ill-wishers of the Government arranged for a meeting, and induced many persons to attend the meeting by false pretences and gave out that a Diwan would be held there. But the people were not informed of the danger in going there.

'About 5 p.m. the General Sahib, with about fifty Indian troops, went to the spot. There was no European soldier with him. Seeing the soldiers, the people showed an attitude of defiance. On this the order to fire was given with the result that many were wounded and many killed.

'The Government is sorry that some innocent persons were seduced by wicked people to go there and got killed. But everyone should bear in mind that obedience to the order of the General Sahib is obligatory, and that the General Sahib will not, in future, put up with any kind of unrest.'

General Dyer was still concerned with the attitude of the Sikhs and the danger of the seduction of his Indian troops by the malcontents who, he learned, had been feeding them with sweetmeats, and on April 16th he journeyed to Lahore to confer with Sir Michael O'Dwyer, the two men most concerned in the suppression of the disturbances meeting for the first time. Asked by O'Dwyer why he went on firing, Dyer said that when he attacked the crowd there was a movement in one direction and he thought they were trying to get behind him. At a conference of officers held at Jullundur, General Dyer was assured that the Indian troops were 'all loyal and were not in sympathy with the disorders'. He returned to Amritsar and on April 19th he paid a visit to the Fort, where he saw Miss Sherwood 'swathed in bandages and lying between life and death'.

Dyer was severely criticized by the Hunter Committee for the 'Crawling Order' which he imposed on people using the street in which Miss Sherwood had been assaulted, an act of humiliation which the Committee found exacerbated racial feeling in Amritsar. Dyer's notorious crawling order, and the reasons he gave for imposing it, and his whipping of the boys *suspected* of the assault on Miss Sherwood, are an indication to his character, and, as they may be a guide to the attitude he adopted in respect to his 'duty' in firing and continuing to fire in the Jallianwala Bagh, his explanations require consideration.

After leaving the Fort, Dyer issued an order closing the street, the *Kucha Kaurhianwala* lane, where Miss Sherwood had been beaten up, and he ordered a triangle to be erected in it for the purpose of whipping those responsible for the outrage. Military pickets were posted at each end of the narrow and very dirty lane with orders that no Indians were to be allowed to pass but, if they insisted, they were to be made to crawl on all fours. Just after Dyer gave the order, some Indians being taken to the police station for failing to salaam him, an act of insolence, were brought to the lane and they were forced to crawl by the picket, and between the 19th and 25th, when the order was withdrawn on Sir Michael O'Dwyer expressing his displeasure, some fifty Indians were made to crawl through the lane.

A number of Indians told the Indian Congress Sub-Committee

of their experiences. Kanyha Lal said that he was struck by the soldiers with the butt-ends of their rifles and forced to crawl on his belly. When he stopped to take breath he was struck again. He saw others made to crawl, including an old, lame man who was kicked and beaten. Labh Chand Seth and his office staff were forced to crawl 'on their bellies like snails'. Anyone who remonstrated, he testified, was knocked down and compelled to crawl, to creep with their bellies touching the ground. No respect was paid to age. A blind beggar was told he could seek food only if he crawled down the lane. Others stated that closing of the lane resulted in an accumulation of filth and rubbish for no sweeper would come to clear it, and that the British soldiers polluted the wells and shot the sacred pigeons. None of the residents were able to go out to obtain the necessities of life for a week.

When the inconvenience to which the residents of the street, none of whom were accused of the assault on Miss Sherwood, was put to General Dyer by the Indian members of the Hunter Committee, he said he thought they could have gone over the roofs of the other houses, a view upon which the minority members expressed the opinion that 'We are unable to understand how General Dyer expected the residents of the houses to go from the roof of one house to another, the houses being of different heights, and thereby reach the street'.

Six Indians, who were described by Major S. R. Shirley, the Provost Marshal, 'as those implicated in the assault', were brought to the street and there whipped, not for the crime of assaulting Miss Sherwood, for which they had not been tried, but for 'gross insubordination and for offering violence while in military custody'.

A triangle was erected in the lane and the whippings were witnessed by its residents, several of whom told the Congress Sub-Committee what they saw, corroborating each other in detail. Each of the six boys was stripped naked, fastened to the triangle and given thirty blows with a heavy cane. Several became unconscious after a few stripes; they were revived with water and the flogging continued. All were bleeding profusely when they were dragged away by the soldiers.

In his report on the matter, contained in his dispatch dated August 25th, General Dyer stated:

'A helpless woman had been mercilessly beaten, in a most cruel manner, by a lot of dastardly cowards. She was beaten with sticks and shoes, and knocked down six times in the street. She tried to gain entrance at an open door, but the door was slammed in her face. To be beaten with shoes is considered by Indians to be the greatest insult. It seemed intolerable to me that some suitable punishment could not be meted out. Civil law was at an end and I searched my brain for some military punishment to meet the case.

'I inspected the spot where Miss Sherwood ultimately fell, and I gave orders for a triangle to be erected there. I then posted two British picquets, one at each end of the street, with orders to allow no Indians to pass, that if they had to pass they must go through on all fours. I never imagined that any sane man would voluntarily go through under those conditions, and I was still searching for some fitting punishment when Providence stepped in. After giving my orders I proceeded further through the city, and as I passed I gave orders for eleven insolent inhabitants to be handed over to the police, and brought to me at the Ram Bagh at 9 a.m. next morning. I did not know that the police who accompanied my force had been left at the far end of the street in which the picquets were posted. Arrived at the near end of the street, the prisoners were confronted by the non-commissioned officer in command of the picquet and made to crawl, between the two picquets, a distance of about 150 yards. I presumed that there were back entrances to the houses which would enable those living in the street to obtain food and water, and it would not take much ingenuity to improvise other means of obtaining the necessities of life. My orders remained in force from the afternoon of the 19th to the 24th of April, 1919. In all some fifty complied with the order to go through on all fours, but I cannot understand why any went through after the 19th, especially as all the houses had back exits and the picquets were only on duty from 6 a.m. to 8 p.m. The only conclusion that I can come to is that, except for the eleven I referred to above, all went through to make martyrs of themselves. Sergeant W. H. Nicholls, 1-25th Battalion, London Regiment, who was in charge of the picquet on all the days, informs me that the extra men came there apparently voluntarily, as they were not brought to him by anybody. One man actually crawled through three times and had to be stopped, by the picquet, from giving further exhibitions.'

Dyer was closely questioned by Lord Hunter and by other

members of the Committee about both his crawling order, and the whippings of the boys. He looked upon all women as being sacred, Dyer said. His object in closing the lane where Miss Sherwood had been assaulted was, he agreed, to punish the guilty. The little inconvenience its residents were forced to suffer was not much in relation to what Amritsar had done. Its people had behaved very badly and the residents of the lane had done nothing to help Miss Sherwood. He thought the place where she had been attacked was 'sacred', and he decided to lash those who had beaten her there. Those who were lashed in the lane were the men who had assaulted her, he stated categorically, an answer which led him into great difficulties when he was required to explain how he knew they were the guilty ones, when they had not been tried for that offence. Dyer agreed they had been lashed 'for some other offence', but he knew they were the ones who had beaten Miss Sherwood, he declared. It was a coincidence that the men lashed for a breach of Fort discipline were also the men who had assaulted her. Everyone knew, he said, that they were the guilty ones. 'I simply lashed them', he explained to Lord Hunter. He especially wanted to punish the men who had committed the assault, he said.

Another member of the Committee, Mr. Justice Rankin, was curious to know how Dyer had decided these particular boys, who had so conveniently committed a breach of discipline while in custody, were the men guilty of the assault. The chances were, from what he had been told, that these were the particular men, Dyer replied. Everyone knew that, and they deserved to be punished. Asked if it was certain, when he ordered them to be whipped, that they would be found guilty of the offence against Miss Sherwood, Dyer made an extraordinary admission. 'I did not know they would be found guilty: when they were *not* found guilty, I lashed them', he stated, which made it sound as if it had been found impossible to produce convincing evidence against them. In reply to an Indian member, Pandit Jayat Narayan, he got into an even worse muddle. If, as had been stated, the authorities came to know on April 23rd who were the persons responsible for the assault, how was it possible, he enquired, that these six men were flogged in the lane *prior to* that date? How did General Dyer *know* they were the persons concerned? Dyer could only reply lamely that information might have been given against them before that date. 'Who informed you?' probed the Government Advocate, Mr Herbert.

'The man who arrested them', replied Dyer. Was it not curious, Mr Herbert suggested, that no other prisoners, except these particular six men, had been punished for breaches of Fort discipline? Was that not an extraordinary coincidence? 'They may have been particularly wicked people', answered Dyer. He admitted that he did not know what offence these men had committed.

Dyer's ill-advised crawling order, and his whipping of the six boys suspected but not convicted of the assault on the woman missionary, suggests that Dyer was a hot-headed man, determined to wreck indiscriminate vengeance on those he believed responsible. Dyer, it seems, was a man easily provoked to outbursts of indignation, even of passion, especially where his own particular foibles were concerned. 'Duty', 'obedience', and the 'sacredness of women', were the basic laws of his existence. The story of the brutal assault on Miss Sherwood infuriated him. The sight of her, swathed in bandages and lying between life and death, enraged him and, in his own words, he searched his brain for a fitting punishment on those responsible, from which he did not exonerate the inhabitants of the street. The lane where the woman had been assaulted was 'sacred', therefore those using it must go on all fours as a mark of respect. He was convinced that the six boys who had been arrested were guilty of the crime. By a remarkable coincidence they committed an unknown breach of discipline. So he had lashed them in the lane. The incident hardly suggests that Dyer was a well-balanced man. He failed to accord these boys the privilege of a person accused under British law, civil or military, to be assumed innocent until proved guilty, the very principle on which he based his claim against his own forced retirement.

When the attention of Sir Michael O'Dwyer was called to the crawling order by the Viceroy, Lord Chelmsford, he replied, 'The order gave me as much of a shock as it did Your Excellency', and he informed him, 'I asked—I could not order—that it should at once be cancelled'. When Dyer came to see him, O'Dwyer noted, 'I think he now realizes the impropriety of the order', and he observed in his memoirs, in respect to the administration of martial law in the Punjab, 'The order in question is the only one I have noticed which indicates serious misuse of authority'. In its dispatch to the Secretary of State, which accompanied the Hunter Report, the Government of India called the crawling order 'highly improper'.

The day on which the crawling order was withdrawn, General Sir William Beynon visited Amritsar, Dyer taking the opportunity to show the Jallianwala Bagh to his superior officer. When Beynon asked why he went on firing, Dyer told him, 'I started firing because I had to. I went on firing because, when I opened fire, they spread out on both sides. Those on the right came surging back, and I thought that they were going over me.' Beynon understood and approved, says Dyer's biographer.

A few days later Dyer was told by the stationmaster at Amritsar that a large consignment of *lathis*, numbering over 200,000, as against a mere 144 in the same period in the preceding year, had arrived by train, information which confirmed Dyer's belief that the rioters had intended to form a bludgeon army.

The situation was now sufficiently calm to enable the authorities to despatch the women and children who had been kept in the Fort for nineteen days to the hills, special trains being run at the cost of Rs.30,000, which was borne by the Army, packed with refugees from Amritsar and Lahore. 'The sight of these trains', says our anonymous Englishwoman, 'must have given residents in unaffected districts some idea of what the riots meant. And yet it has been stated that there was no real insecurity and no more trouble than the police could have dealt with. No European who was in Amritsar or Lahore doubts that for some days there was a very real danger of the entire European population being massacred, and that General Dyer's action alone saved them.'

VIII

MARTIAL LAW

The riots, revolt or rebellion in the Punjab, depending upon the particular point of view, had been crushed. There remained only the task of punishing the offenders, one which the British administrators, civil and military, set about with typical national thoroughness, even ruthlessly, if the statements made to the Indian Congress Sub-Committee are to be believed. Charges of barbarous treatment were made by many of the 1,700 witnesses examined by Gandhi and his associates. Clearly their testimony must be taken with caution, for it now cannot be tested and it may have been tinged with animosity against the national oppressors. On the other hand, we need to bear in mind that, if these charges had been made against the Nazis in Europe, we would probably have accepted them without reservation. It is a matter of who are the oppressed and who the oppressors. We may note, however, that the Hunter Committee found that the administration of martial law was 'marred in particular instances by a misuse of power, by irregularities, and injudicious and irresponsible acts' and it observed 'it was not being administered in an enemy country but in a country where, on the restoration of normal conditions, it was advisable that martial law administration should leave behind as little feeling of bitterness and unfairness as possible'.

The administration of martial law in the Central Punjab, particularly the acts of certain individuals, came in for severe criticism by a number of Indians, who made specific charges of undue severity and disregard of legal and moral principles.

General Dyer's crawling order and his whipping of 'suspects' cannot be considered in isolation and for a proper assessment of his character they need to be compared with the acts of other officials.

Complaints were made by Indians of excessive and brutal punishment, wrongful and illegal arrests, 'frame-ups', blackmail to induce false evidence, long internments without charges, intimidation and harsh treatment in prison. There were 'many high-handed acts', states Sir Sankaran Nair, then a member of the Government of India, in his book (which led to Sir Michael O'Dwyer's action for libel in 1924) *Gandhi and Anarchy*. A total of 270 floggings were administered, a recognized form of punishment under both civil and military legal codes, the value of which, says Mr Jayakar, the British considered as 'equal to one thousand soldiers in keeping the peace'. Corporal punishment was much resented by Indians, who considered it degrading, and sentences of from five to thirty lashes with a cane, and with a lash in Kasur, were inflicted for such minor crimes as failing to salaam, breaches of the curfew order, disrespect to Europeans, selling milk, and for no crime at all except that certain individuals were chosen as examples. The Hunter Committee Majority Members found that some of the sentences imposed were excessive and others were open to criticism, and the minority considered there had been an unwise resort to flogging and that its scale must have resulted in bitterness.

Sentences of whipping under the Martial Law Regulations were carried out in Lahore (80), Kasur (85), Chuharkam (40), Gujranwala (24), Gurat (3), Amritsar (38). At the start the floggings were administered in public, but on the order of the Viceroy this was discontinued, to the apparent displeasure of one administrator who told the Hunter Committee 'when the civil population runs amuck, if I may say so, as in this case, it is the only method by which you can deal with it'.

As well as these punishments for minor crimes, 581 people were convicted in Lahore of waging war against the King Emperor, and 108 were sentenced to death, 265 to transportation for life, 2 to transportation for fixed periods, 5 to imprisonment for ten years, 85 for seven years and 104 for shorter periods. The Provincial Government maintained 23 death sentences, reducing the others to periods of imprisonment, ranging from life to five years. Many of these convicted persons were amnested by Royal Pardon at the end of 1919.

Several incidents may be compared with General Dyer's crawling order.

General Campbell's salaaming order in Gujranwala was criticized by the Hunter Committee, which observed that 'no good object was served by making all Indians, whatever their station, show these remarks of respect to all Commissioned Officers'. The order, which opened with the statement, 'Whereas it has come to my notice that certain inhabitants are habitually exhibiting a lack of respect', required all Indians riding in conveyances to alight, and those carrying umbrellas to lower them, and to salute all officers with the hand.

Captain Doveton at Kasur was criticized both by the Hunter Committee and by individual Indians. The Committee admonished him for making minor offenders skip and compose poems in praise of martial law and for subjecting all convicted offenders to undue humiliation by touching the ground with their foreheads, a form of punishment which led to wild rumours, it being said that a respected Sadhu had been forced to draw pictures in the dust with his nose. Asked by members of the Committee what he intended to accomplish by this, Captain Doveton answered, 'The main object was to impress on the people that everybody was not his own master and they had got to conform to orders'. He thought it was a suitable punishment, he declared. A number of Indians who gave evidence to the Congress Sub-Committee stated they had been flogged, at Captain Doveton's order, in the presence of prostitutes, which degraded them, and eight dancing girls testified they had been forced to watch the floggings, made to inspect the bleeding bodies and were warned 'observe carefully the result of love-making'. It is not exactly stated for what crime these men were punished, the implication being that they were caught in the girls' house after curfew

Another incident which occurred in Kasur was not laid to Captain Doveton's door. A number of students were paraded and their headmaster was ordered, states the Hunter Committee Report, to pick six boys to be flogged. When those he selected appeared to be 'miserable looking', the Sub-Divisional Officer ordered the whole school to be paraded before Lieutenant Colonel Macrae, who was questioned by the Committee thus:

Q. Then on the 18th, some schoolboys were flogged and you gave directions that the six biggest boys were to be selected for that purpose?

A. I said generally speaking, take the six biggest. The misfortune was that they happened to be big.

Q. It was irrespective of whether they were innocent or guilty; because they were big they had to suffer?

A. Yes.

Q. Do you think that is a reasonable thing to do?

A. Yes, I think so under certain circumstances.

Q. It was a mere accident that a boy being big should invite on himself punishment?

A. It was his misfortune.

Each of the boys was given six lashes with a cane.

A headman at a place near Kasur who was unable to give information to Mr S. M. Jacob, Director of Agriculture, about the cutting of telegraph wires, was bound to a tree and given fifteen lashes, it being learnt subsequently that the wires had been cut in another village.

Colonel Frank Johnson, Martial Law Administrator at Lahore, was criticized by individual Indians who complained that he commandeered vehicles owned by Indians, and by the Committee for saying that he did so as 'I wanted to teach them a lesson'. Several others, barristers, told the Congress Sub-Committee that they had been arrested on no charge and were held in prison under horrible conditions for long periods, and testimony was given by several medical practitioners who claimed they had been forced to divulge the names of those whose wounds they had treated, so that they might be arrested. More specific charges were made by owners of property who alleged that martial law notices had been posted on their buildings solely to punish them by forcing them to guard the posters from being defaced or torn down. Questioned about this, Colonel Johnson told the Hunter Committee he had selected the premises of those who were suspected to be not 'very loyal', and when he was asked if he thought the measure revealed its punitive nature, and was not therefore reasonable, he answered, 'Quite. I would do it again. It was one of the few brainwaves I had.' He agreed that when he learned that a notice had been torn down at the Dharam College, he ordered the arrest of sixty-five students and the professors, all of whom were made to march three miles and stand all day in the sun. He said he had been awaiting an opportunity to show the students the power of martial law and he took this opportunity to do so. On his attention being called to another incident, when he ordered a number of students to march seventeen miles a day in the heat of the sun to answer roll calls, he protested it was only sixteen miles. He had consulted the map, he stated, and he explained that it was 'no hardship for able-bodied young men. It was only a mild type of physical exercise.' The order, he told the Committee, was not passed as a punishment but to keep the students out of mischief.

Some students were expelled and declared unfit to enter other colleges, it was alleged. The Committee found Colonel Johnson's order 'unnecessarily severe'.

Several other Indians cited incidents of similar 'undue severity' to the Congress Sub-Committee. Malik Mohammed Husain said that a military officer struck him with a hunting crop. He raised his arm to protect himself. He was arrested for 'opposing a military officer' and sentenced to receive twenty lashes. Lala Parasram, a cloth merchant, was given five lashes for being out of his house after curfew, his excuse that he went to get milk for his child being rejected. Lala Tota Ram, a milk-seller, was flogged unconscious and sentenced to three months imprisonment for allegedly selling milk above the fixed price. Lala Tulsi Ram alleged he was flogged on false evidence given by a neighbour who bribed a constable to arrest him.

Ganesh Das witnessed floggings in the municipal market in Lahore. He told the Congress Committee, 'The scene of the flogging was quite heart-rending; people who were flogged cried and shrieked and the sight was horrible. Their clothes were stripped off, and their hands were tied to the flogging post. The Europeans standing round felt very much delighted and shouted "Strike hard, strike more".' He said that 'The people after being flogged became senseless'. Mian Alla Bux, who watched the floggings, said that English ladies present were smiling. One of those flogged, Pandit Khushal Chand, saw Englishwomen watching.

When a mobile column visited a village near Kasur, an entire wedding party was arrested for breach of the curfew order and 'more than ten' were whipped, according to the Hunter Committee Report, which states that in passing sentence on one of them the Area Officer declared, 'He is young. Flogging will do him good.'

These 'fancy punishments', indiscriminate floggings, and the over-exuberant enthusiasm for exacting retribution for the outrages committed by a subject people, show that Dyer was not the only British officer who acted in a vindictive manner. His crawling order and his whippings of suspects achieved greater prominence than the no less discreditable acts of other officials because they were done by General Dyer, the hero of the hour, or the villain of the piece, whichever way the reader of the evidence considered him. It is clear that a number of British officials, including Dyer, behaved indiscreetly in the administration of martial law in the Punjab, a period which Mr Jawaharlal

Nehru, in his autobiography, calls one of 'long horror and terrible indignity'. Retribution and punishment were the orders of the day and in their infliction the British officers showed themselves only too human. Martial law continued in the Punjab until June 6th. 'The Punjab', says Mr Nehru, 'was isolated, cut off from the rest of India; a thick veil seemed to cover it, and hide it from outside eyes. There was hardly any news and people could not go there or come out from there.' Odd individuals, he states, who managed to escape from 'that inferno' were so terror-struck that they could give no clear account.

Living in the Punjab was a boy of sixteen, named Udham Singh. He heard about the indignities inflicted on his people and of the shooting in the Jallianwala Bagh. His mind became inflamed against the British and he did not forget.

IX

DYER REPORTS

'The tragedy of the Jallianwala Bagh was staggering for its dramatic effect', states the Report of the Indian Congress Sub-Committee.

Did Dyer's act quell a riot or crush a rebellion? The Afghan War which flared up on the North West Frontier in May 1919 was taken by Sir Michael O'Dwyer to confirm his belief that the 'rebellion', as he termed the disorders, in the Punjab was the result of an organized conspiracy intended to synchronize with the Afghan invasion, a master plan which had gone off 'half-cock'.

The Afghans, says O'Dwyer, 'were encouraged by the belief that the Punjab was teething with rebellion and ready to receive them with open arms', but 'instead of being welcomed by mutinous troops and a rebellious population, as they had been led to expect, they found a well-equipped army of two hundred thousand men barring their way, supported by the loyal millions of the rural Punjab'. The 'rebellion' had been crushed before 'our external enemies were ready', he says and he observes that the Afghans 'began a concerted attack on the North West Frontier *at the end* of April', a fact which 'though well known was never brought out before the Hunter Committee'.

The Hunter Committee, O'Dwyer says, refused to consider any evidence of connection between the Punjab rebellion and the Afghan invasion. 'Had they done so', he declares, 'they would have hesitated to put on record the extraordinary view that "*on the evidence before us there is nothing to show that the outbreak in the Punjab was part of a pre-arranged conspiracy to overthrow the British Government in India by force*".'

As well as being a pointer to the question whether the Punjab disorders were a 'riot' or a 'rebellion', which may influence our assessment of Dyer's action in the Jallianwala Bagh, the Afghan War, the third of that series, has another interest for us, for Dyer took part in it and, by his relief of Thal, earned 'great credit', in the words of the dispatch of the Commander-in-Chief, Sir Charles Monro.

Dyer and his 45th Brigade were ordered to join General Beynon's 16th Division on the frontier and he reached Peshawar on May 28th. 'I had by then become aware', he said in his statement to the Army Council on July 3, 1920, 'that the influences which had inspired the rebellion were starting an agitation against those who had suppressed it.' At his first interview with the Commander at Peshawar, General Sir Arthur Barrett, he told him, 'I wish, if possible, to be free from any anxiety about my action at Amritsar, which so far had been approved'. 'That's all right', replied Barrett. 'You would have heard about it long before this if your action had not been approved.'

Relieved of further anxiety by these words, Dyer marched his Brigade into enemy territory and on June 1st he drove off the Afghan army investing the town of Thal, in which a British force was beleaguered. But strains and exertions of the operation, which was carried out in a shade temperature of 120 degrees, broke Dyer's health, states his biographer, who tells us: 'Strong as it was, his constitution had been undermined by the fevers and suns of that terrible climate. In the very act of dictating his orders for the decisive attack on the heights above Thal he had fallen down in an agony of pain, and had only been restored by the aspirin and brandy which, by doctor's orders, his devoted Brigade-Major carried with him as a precaution against such an emergency.'

Dyer, records Mr Colvin, was brought back to Peshawar, where he received Sir Charles Monro's congratulations, without there being any word of censure about his action at Amritsar. He was given ten days' leave at Dalhousie, and on August 2nd he was called to Simla, where Sir Charles Monro ordered him to write a report on his action at Amritsar.

Nothing had so far been said which might have caused Dyer to doubt that his superiors approved his action in the Jallianwala Bagh. There was not a cloud on the horizon. When, on May 22nd, the Secretary of State for India, Mr Montagu, spoke in the House of Commons of the events of April, he made no reference to the Jallianwala Bagh, and his words seemed to support the views of Dyer and O'Dwyer, for he referred to the disorders as 'rebellion and revolution', and he went on to say: 'The danger is not past; it exists. It is not something that is finished; it threatens'. He took the view, apparently, that there was a conspiracy behind the rebellion. 'Evidence accumulates every day that there is in India a small body of men who are the enemies of the Government, men who any government, bureaucratic or democratic, alien or idigenous, if it is worth the name of government, must deal with.' An enquiry there must be, declared Mr Montagu, but 'let us talk of an enquiry when the fire is put out', he said, and he concluded his speech with these words:

'The only message we send out from this House today to India is a message of confidence and sympathy with those upon whom the great responsibility has fallen to restore the situation. Then will come the time to hold an enquiry, not only to help us to remove the causes, but in order to dispose, once for all, of some of the libellous charges which had been made against British troops and those upon whom the unpleasant duties in connection with these riots have fallen.'

Says Mr Colvin: 'General Dyer could hardly have supposed from these heartening words, as he wiped the sweat of the conflagration from his brow, that the trial of the firemen had only been postponed until after they had put out the fire'.

Confident that his action had been correct, Dyer returned to Dalhousie to write his report.

Unknown to Dyer, powerful forces were massing against him. As the news of the casualties in the Jallianwala Bagh leaked out, it sent a 'thrill of horror' throughout the province, according to Dr Gokal Chand Narang, a barrister in Lahore. For some weeks the Martial Law Regulation, which forbade entry into the Punjab and censured the press, prevented the news spreading through India but, with the abolition of the order on June 6th, the story of how the unarmed and unresisting crowd, penned in an enclosure, had been shot down was carried everywhere. Hundreds of people had been killed without warning, it was rumoured. Resentment of British rule became more pronounced and Mr Leonard Mosley (*The Last Days of the British Raj*) states, 'What is certain is that the Amritsar shootings turned most Indians, including those who had co-operated willingly before, into resentful and mistrustful minions, conscious that the British who ruled them regarded their lives as unimportant and their race as inferior', and he calls the Jallianwala Bagh 'the greatest recruiting poster for Congress ever to be waved before the Indian people'. He says that 'they joined up in their thousands'.

Indian antagonism was aroused at the moment when the Government of India and the Secretary of State in London were particularly anxious to appease the agitators in order to gain their co-operation in the proposed Montagu-Chelmsford reforms, which were soon to be put in operation. 'I had no sooner left India', says Sir Michael O'Dwyer, 'than a violent agitation, enforced by every form of calumny and misrepresentation, was set on foot in India and in England to vilify all those who had helped to crush the rebellion, and to prevent future resort to "the speedy and effective methods of martial law".' The Government of India, he says, feared that this fictitious agitation might disturb the peaceful atmosphere they desired, and they gave way to it, 'instead of boldly following up the advantage gained by the suppression of the rebellion'. They adopted a weak defensive position, states O'Dwyer. 'The Indian extremists, as usual, seeing that they again had the Government on the run, redoubled their attacks, and sedulously spread the false and malicious propaganda which gradually consolidated into the "Punjab atrocities".' And he adds that the Secretary of State 'was only too ready to conciliate Indian opinion by lending ear to the tales of the Indian politicians who had swarmed into London in the summer of 1919'.

O'Dwyer himself, when he reached London in June, had a long interview with the Secretary of State at which, he says, he gave Mr Montagu full information about the outbreak in the Punjab.

In Dalhousie, Dyer worked on his report, handicapped, his biographer says, by the absence of Captain Briggs, his Brigade-Major. Dyer's dispatch, addressed to the 'General Staff, 16th (Indian) Division' and dated August 25th, represents his first attempt to justify his action in the Jallianwala Bagh. He was now on the defensive, it seems. Although his action had been officially approved, he was aware that it had been called into question in certain quarters.

Dyer started by emphasizing the necessity of mentioning certain events which occurred prior to April 11th in order to show why 'I considered it my bounden duty to disperse by rifle fire the unlawful assembly in the Jallianwala Bagh'. He cites various trivial examples, the insubordinate behaviour of certain Sepoys in 1918 and early in 1919, to show that 'when possible I used my best endeavour to suppress riotous crowds without the use of unnecessary force'. But at Amritsar 'the case was very different', he observes. The crowd defied him. It forced his hand. The city was in a state of complete lawlessness. From a military point of view there was every reason for him to open fire. He referred to the events that preceded his action. How his car was attacked in Delhi and on his return to Jullundur, a tour which thoroughly impressed him 'with the dangerous nature of the feelings of the inhabitants'. The code telegram received which told him trouble was expected in Amritsar. How he sent more troops than ordered, because he felt the situation was very bad. His arrival in Amritsar. The information he was given about the murders and the dastardly attacks on individuals. The news that the telegraph wires and railway lines had been cut. That the mob had taken the law into their own hands; that the situation was beyond civil control. That he was invited to take charge. The inhabitants of the surrounding villages were pouring into the city, swelling the ranks of the mob, which was forming itself into a 'bludgeon army'. When he marched his column into the city, it was greeted by insolence, by cries of 'Hindus and Muslims unite'. He considered the advisability of opening fire. He came to the conclusion that he should issue a personal proclamation before taking such drastic measures. On the morning of the 13th he marched through the city, making his proclamation at all important streets, warning that crowds would be fired on, whereupon the people clapped their hands and laughingly proclaimed, 'This is only bluff and no firing will take place'. Hotfoot on his proclamation, a counter proclamation was issued declaring, 'The British Raj is at an end', and 'Not to be afraid of being fired on'. He was informed that, in spite of his stern proclamation, a big meeting would be held at that afternoon. At 4.30 p.m. he proceeded to the Jallianwala Bagh with all the troops available, dropping picketing parties as he marched.

Dyer recalled his knowledge of the situation then existing both in Amritsar and the Punjab, and his fear that he might be completely isolated. He had made a proclamation that morning and there was no reason to parley further with the mob, for they were evidently there to defy the law. Open rebellion reigned in Amritsar and it was his duty to suppress it.

The next passage needs to be considered in detail for, as we shall learn later, Dyer also gave other reasons for firing upon the assembly.

'The responsibility was very great. If I fired I must fire with good effect, a small amount of firing would be a criminal act of folly.

'I had the choice of carrying out a very distasteful and horrible duty or of neglecting to do my duty, of suppressing disorder or of becoming responsible for all future bloodshed.

'We cannot be very brave unless we be possessed of a greater fear. I had considered the matter from every point of view. My duty and my military instincts told me to fire. My conscience was also clear on that point. What faced me was, what on the morrow would be the *Danda Fauj*.

'I fired and continued to fire until the crowd dispersed and I consider this the least amount of firing which would produce the necessary moral, and widespread effect it was my duty to produce, if I was to justify my action. If more troops had been at hand the casualties would have been greater in proportion. It *was no longer a question of merely dispersing the crowd*; but one of producing a sufficient moral effect, from a military point of view, not only on those who were present but more specially throughout the Punjab. There could be no question of undue severity.'

'Many inhabitants', he said, 'thanked me and recognized that I had committed a just and merciful act', and he related that on later days he was thanked by thousands, the press of people being greater than the Court House grounds could hold. He did not offer help to the wounded, he said, after the shooting was over, 'because the military situation had to be considered throughout the incident'. He went on, 'The crowd was so dense that if a determined rush had been made at any time, arms or no arms, my small force must instantly have been overpowered and consequently I was very careful of not giving the mob a chance of organizing. I sometimes ceased fire and redirected my fire where the crowd was collecting more thickly. By the time I had completely dispersed the crowd my ammunition was running short. I returned to the Ram Bagh without counting or inspecting the casualties. The crowd was free now to ask for medical aid, but this they avoided doing lest they themselves be proved to have attended the assembly.'

Continuing his report, Dyer went on to say, 'Had prompt measures not been taken on the 13th and had the Punjab Government not expressed their approval of this and other strong measures such as those initiated at Lahore by Colonel Frank Johnson, I am strongly of opinion that acts of violence, plunder and bloodshed would immediately have been perpetrated on a much larger scale through India'.

The Honorary Magistrates, the leading citizens and the

Municipal Councillors of the city, he stated, expressed their admiration for his firm action and told him he had saved Amritsar and the other cities of the Punjab from complete plunder and bloodshed.

Dyer stressed the efforts he had made to prevent the Sikhs from joining the mutineers, saying, 'I was born in India and had served in Punjab Regiments all my service, I know the language very well and I consider I am an authority on what was going on in and around Amritsar'. He stated, 'The effect of the events on April 13 and these movements (the mobile columns he sent round the villages) snatched the villagers from the hands of the agitators'.

He proceeded from Amritsar to the North West Frontier on May 8th, Dyer stated, and, he pointed out, 'Had the situation in the Punjab not been promptly and firmly dealt with in April, telegraph and railway lines would in all probability have been damaged to a much greater extent and concentration on the Frontier against the Afghans rendered very difficult if not impossible, and the situation would have been most critical'.

Dyer made no suggestion in his report of there being an emergency or anything in the demeanour of the crowd in the Jallianwala Bagh which compelled him to fire at once without warning. He meant to fire and he meant to kill in order to teach a lesson and create an impression. The act was not forced on him; he did it deliberately. He had two objects; to punish the crowd and to give warning to others.

He sent his report to Simla and awaited events. There was as yet no cloud on Dyer's horizon. He was still the Hero of the Hour, the man who had saved the Punjab from even greater bloodshed and all India, perhaps, from a second Mutiny, that terrible bugbear which had haunted the thoughts of the white rulers of India for sixty years; the fear that blinded them to the truth, established by five hundred years of history, that millions of unarmed natives are no match for a few resolute men armed with guns.

X

THE SOLDIER

General Dyer had shot down a crowd of unresisting Indians, killing 379, the figure arrived at by the Allahabad Social Service League after an investigation held in August. The number of injured was estimated at 1,200, but it was found impossible to check this figure, because few of the wounded reported the fact for fear of being arrested as participants in the unlawful assembly. Dyer had fired without warning and he had continued firing for ten minutes, the Government of India learned from his report, the first detailed information they received of the 'actual circumstances', Lord Chelmsford stated in 1924. The April disturbances had resulted in a number of other deaths, Indian and European, and British thoroughness required that the disorders be investigated and their cause ascertained. In October it was announced that a Committee of Enquiry, presided over by Lord Hunter, a Scottish High Court judge, would take evidence at Delhi and in the Punjab, and report. In addition to Lord Hunter, the Committee was composed of four Europeans and three Indians:

> The Honourable Mr Justice G. C. Rankin, Judge of the High Court, Calcutta.
> The Honourable Mr W. F. Rice, C.S.I., I.C.S., Additional Secretary to the Government of India, Home Department.
> Major-General Sir George Barrow, K.C.B., K.C.M.G., I.A., Commanding the Peshawar Division.
> The Honourable Pandit Jagat Narayan, B.A., Member of the Legislative Council of the Lieutenant-Governor of the United Provinces.
> The Honourable Mr Thomas Smith, Member of the Legislative Council of the Lieutenant-Governor of the United Provinces.
> Sir Chimanlal Harilal Setalvad, Kt., Advocate of the High Court, Bombay.
> Sardar Sahibzada Sultan Ahmed Khan, Muntazim-ud-Doula, M.A., LL.M.(Cantab), Barrister at Law, Member for Appeals, Gwalior State.

The All India Congress Committee, invited by Lord Hunter to submit evidence, refused on the ground that the Government would not allow the principal Punjab leaders, who were in prison, to appear. In consequence, the Congress Sub-Committee was set up independently to hear evidence under the presidency of Gandhi.

Meanwhile General Dyer had rejoined his 45th Brigade, now stationed at Chahlala, six miles from Rawalpindi. A month later, the Brigade, says Mr Colvin, was ordered to Bannu 'without General Dyer, who was to take another command'. He was ordered to Peshawar and given the 5th Brigade, with his headquarters at Jamrud Fort, at the mouth of the Khyber Pass, 'a command', says Mr Colvin, 'which suggested to him that he enjoyed the confidence as well as the gratitude of the Commander-in-Chief'. General Beynon's report on the activities of his division during the disturbances in April, written on September 5th, shows that Dyer's immediate superior continued the support he had accorded him in April, for he states that 'The wisdom of General Dyer's action has been fully proved by the fact that there has been no further trouble in Amritsar', and he added that 'The strong measures taken by General Dyer at Amritsar had a far reaching effect and prevented any further trouble in the Lahore Divisional Area'. Beynon went even further in his support of Dyer in 1924. Giving evidence in the libel case brought by Sir Michael O'Dwyer, he described Dyer's action as 'perfectly correct'. He was more than ever convinced of it, he declared emphatically. He gave his opinion that, if Dyer had not opened fire, his force would have been wiped out in two minutes. He had to act immediately.

Shortly after taking up his new appointment, Dyer received a further reassurance that his action was officially approved. The Indemnity Bill, framed (according to established practice) to protect officials who had acted under the Martial Law Regulations, came up for discussion in the Legislative Council on September 19th. Sir Michael O'Dwyer states, 'Pandit Malivya and others, who for months had been carrying on a virulent campaign against the Punjab Government and the officials who had crushed the rebellion, came forward with the wildest allegations against my misdeeds and Dyer's action at Amritsar', and he says that their actions were defended and justified in a most powerful and convincing speech by the Adjutant-General, Sir Havelock Hudson.

Dealing with the firing in the Jallianwala Bagh, the Adjutant-General outlined the situation in Amritsar as it appeared to General Dyer, a situation of 'utmost gravity', he emphasized. The city was in the hands of an unruly mob, the lives of Europeans had been taken and it was clear to the Officer in Command that the rebellion was not confined to Amritsar alone. He was aware of the danger of the spread of rebellion to the surrounding districts. As an officer in a highly responsible position, Dyer knew that it was his duty to take all measures necessary to restore order and that 'his actions would be judged by the measure of his success in doing so'. He would know also that he would be held personally responsible for any action of his which might be considered in excess of the reasonable requirements of the situation. Sir Havelock Hudson emphasized 'You cannot conceive that any officer on whom such responsibility has been thrown would enter on his task with any spirit of lightheartedness; nor would an officer of his seniority and experience (he had thirty-four years' service) set about his task with a disregard of the sanctity of human life, or with a desire to exact reprisals for the acts of the rebellion which had already been committed'. The Adjutant-General pointed out that the commander's first act would be to dispose his troops with a view to the protection of life and property and his second would be to warn the populace as to the result, if it became necessary, to use military force in the suppression of further disorder. Dyer took both steps, he stressed.

On the 11th and 12th, the speaker observed, Dyer pursued a policy of patience and conciliation and on the 13th he issued his proclamation announcing that unlawful assemblies would be dispersed by fire, a warning which was greeted by jeers, indicating that the mob had no belief in the sincerity of the warning given. Then Dyer learned of the meeting being held in the Jallianwala Bagh, the place where large meetings on March 29th and 30th and April 2nd had listened to speeches intended to bring the Government into hatred and contempt. 'It would have been clear to the Officer in Command that he might expect deliberate defiance of his orders', Sir Havelock Hudson pointed out, stressing the smallness of the force Dyer had at his disposal. 'Realizing the gravity of the situation', he remarked, the Officer Commanding did not send, as he might have done, a subaltern in charge of this small force. He realized it was an occasion on which he, and he alone, must exercise the full responsibility.'

On reaching the Bagh, Dyer's force was confronted by a vast assembly. The Honourable Pandit (Malivya) 'would have us to believe', said the Adjutant-General, 'that this was a fortuitous meeting of villagers and they were listening to a lecture'. That was not in accordance with the facts, he declared. It was clearly the duty of the Officer in Command to disperse the unlawful assembly. 'Realizing the danger to his small force unless he took immediate action, and being well aware of the inadequacy of the measures taken to restore order on April 10th', Dyer ordered fire to be opened.

'I have given the Council this narrative', stated Sir Havelock Hudson, 'to show how the situation would be viewed by the soldier and I will content myself with saying that, from a military point of view, the sequence of events justified the exercise of military force, and that the object of its exercise was attained. Also, from the purely military point of view, the Officer in Command would have been gravely at fault had he permitted the elements of disorder to continue unchecked for a moment longer.'

Sir Havelock Hudson concluded his speech with these emphatic words:

'No more distasteful or responsible duty falls to the lot of the soldier than that which he is sometimes required to discharge in aid of the civil power. If his measures are too mild he fails in his duty. If they are deemed to be excessive he is liable to be attacked as a cold-blooded murderer. His position is one demanding the highest degree of sympathy from all reasonable and right-minded citizens. He is frequently called upon to act on the spur of the moment in grave situations in which he intervenes because all the other resources of civilization have failed. His actions are liable to be judged by *ex post facto* standards, and by persons who are in complete ignorance of the realities which he had to face. His good faith is liable to be impugned by the very persons connected with the organization of the disorders which his action has foiled. There are those who will admit that a measure of force may have been necessary, but who cannot agree with the extent of the force employed. How can they be in a better position to judge of that than the officer on the spot? It must be remembered that when a rebellion has been started against the Government, it is tantamount to a declaration of war. War cannot be conducted in accordance with standards of humanity to which we are accustomed in peace. Should not officers and men, who through no choice of their own, are called upon to discharge these distasteful duties, be in all fairness accorded that support which has been promised to them?'

There it was. Unqualified approval and support from a member of the Government of India, from the Adjutant-General himself, a senior member of the Army High Command. The words Dyer had been waiting to hear for six months. 'Up to this stage', says Sir Michael O'Dwyer, 'everything indicated that Army Headquarters and the Government of India, being in full possession of all the material facts, approved of General Dyer's action just as much as Major-General Beynon and I approved of it on April 14th.'

Privately, Dyer was warned that he would be called as a witness by the 'Punjab Disorders Inquiry Committee'. With these assurances of official support ringing in his ears, he could look forward to the result with confidence. None the less he 'brooded over this matter', General Beynon stated in the evidence he gave at the libel action in 1924. There was nothing to fear, apparently. His record as a soldier was a fine one, Dyer knew.

Reginald Dyer was born on October 9, 1864, at Simla where his father, Edward, had established a brewery and had prospered while catering for the raging thirsts of Hindustan. A second generation Anglo-Indian, for his father had been a pilot in the service of the East India Company, Edward sired nine children, of whom Reginald was the youngest of five sons.

On leaving the school in Ireland to which he had been sent, Rex went to London to cram for Sandhurst, passing out in July 1885 with 'proficiency in Military Law and Tactics', and he was gazetted to the Second Battalion, the Queen's Royal West Surrey Regiment on August 28th. The Second Battalion being then in India, he was posted to the First Battalion in Ireland, one of his brother officers being Charles Monro, six years his senior, who became Commander-in-Chief in India in 1916, a post he held at the time of the Amritsar shooting and its aftermath. In 1885, the two young men became friends, says Mr Colvin, who recalls the tradition that Dyer gave Monro lessons in boxing. 'Thirty-five years later these two were to meet again and hold a short and tragic conversation', he observes.

In October 1886 Dyer sailed to join the Second Battalion in Burma, where war had broken out and he was occupied in the subjugation of the country until the following August, when he went on leave to India, returning to the family home at Simla. In the same year he transferred to the 39th Bengal Infantry, and became engaged to the Colonel's daughter, Anne Ommaney, moves which displeased his parents who hoped he would take a commission in a crack British cavalry regiment. He married on April 4, 1888, and, on the disbandment of the 39th Bengal Infantry, he was appointed Wing Officer in the 29th Punjab Infantry.

Dyer's career in the Indian Army was typical of the period: hard work, regimental duties, an occasional frontier clash, station social life and tours through India, on one of which he and his wife visited Amritsar, sightseeing in a *ghari* and climbing a minaret from where they had a bird's eye view of the Golden Temple, seeing beyond it a dusty open space which, if they had enquired, they would have been told was named the Jallianwala Bagh. Dyer, says his biographer, had a gift for languages; soon after returning to India he passed the Urdu Higher Examination and he spoke Hindustani like a native. He learnt also Persian, Pushtu, the language of the hills, and Punjabee, the latter so well that his bearer laughingly said, 'Nothing is hidden from the Sahib'. From the recollection of his friends, at this time, says Mr Colvin, Dyer 'emerges as a man rather big in build and of remarkable bodily strength, very clever with his hands, and an eternal smoker of cigarettes, often carried in empty envelopes or loose in the pocket; of an absent-minded and casual habit in ordinary life; always deep in some absorbing subject, paying no heed to the small conventions of society, but forgiven all these little sins by reason of an engaging frankness, a perpetual overflow of merriment and good nature'.

Slowly but inevitably Dyer climbed the ladder of promotion. In 1893 he was a Captain, ten years later a Major, and in that period he visited England twice, entering and passing out of the Staff College at Camberley, where his contemporaries included the future Earl Haig and Viscount Allenby. By 1908 he was second-in-command of the 25th Punjabis, and on the outbreak of the World War was promoted Colonel, commanding the Field Force which marched to Sarhad in Baluchistan in 1916 to counteract the German propaganda which was designed to foster anti-British sentiments amongst the tribesmen, an expedition which Dyer describes in his book *The Raiders of the Sarhad*.

As a reward, no doubt, for his excellent handling of the

campaign, Dyer was promoted a temporary Brigadier-General and given command of the 45th Brigade stationed at Jullundur.

From Mr Colvin's account of Dyer's life, he emerges as the best type of Anglo-Indian, a soldier born and bred in India, speaking the languages of the people, understanding them and well liked, a man of charm and varied accomplishments (for he invented an artillery range finder), courteous, humane, capable and determined, a little obtuse perhaps, a typical representative of his class and time, a soldier who had learned to obey orders and who expected others to do the same, a man whose life hinged on his sense of duty, the compelling force which regulated his conduct, a stern conception which allowed no deviation. The man who had no doubts of his duty when he faced the dark dilemma of the Jallianwala Bagh. But not the man to parry the thrusts of the inquisitors of the Disorders Committee, Indian lawyers who, General Beynon observes, 'did not give Dyer a chance'.

XI

ENQUIRY

The Hunter Committee heard the evidence of witnesses on eight days in Delhi, twenty-nine days in Lahore and three days at Bombay. All, with the exception of Sir Michael O'Dwyer, General Hudson and Sir Umar Hayat Khan, a Punjab Government supporter, who gave their evidence *in camera*, being examined in public. Dyer was questioned at Lahore on November 19th. He made a wretched witness, falling into the pitfalls set for the unwary, being goaded to make indiscreet answers and into explaining his action at Amritsar by statements which Sir Michael O'Dwyer, who heard him, found 'indefensible' and which caused him to think, he told the jury at his action for libel in 1924, that Dyer's explanations could not be correct, an opinion confirmed by General Beynon who said on the same occasion, 'I am sorry to say that the evidence he gave is quite different from what he was thinking and doing at the time'.

Ian Colvin states that Dyer had neither friend nor counsel to aid him, and the *Morning Post*, which took up the cudgels on Dyer's behalf, declared at the time of his death, 'the soldier, himself, undefended by counsel was subjected without warning to the cross-examination of lawyers and was thus denied the rights which would have been given to a criminal'.

Sir George Barrow, in his *Life of Sir Charles Monro*, denies this. He says:

'It would be interesting to know who it was denied Dyer the assistance of counsel. It was certainly not the Government of India, nor the Commander-in-Chief, nor the Hunter Committee. On the contrary, counsel was pressed on Dyer by the Government; and his friends, knowing his tendency to excitability, begged him to accept the assistance that was offered to him. Dyer obstinately refused, saying he would and could conduct his own case. Neither was he cross-examined without warning. He had many days in which to prepare his evidence. As to friends ready to help him, they, too, were not wanting. The author of the *Life of General Dyer* himself mentions that Beynon gave Dyer a friendly hint as he was going into the room where the Committee sat. And there was a friend on the Committee itself who was only too anxious to extend to him all the assistance that was possible, but Dyer never gave him a chance. Dyer was at liberty to employ the services of counsel or any of his friends in that capacity.

General Beynon's 'friendly hint', he stated in evidence in 1924, consisted in 'warning Dyer to be careful in his statements, to tell the truth and not to start talking' and he warned him he was up against three of the cleverest Indian lawyers. 'I have no fear', replied Dyer as he went into the room in which the Committee was sitting.

'Enough has been said', remarks Sir George Barrow, 'to disclose the methods which have been resorted to in order to create the impression that Dyer did not receive a fair hearing before the Hunter Committee', a point of view made perhaps a little suspect by Beynon's statement that 'It was not an enquiry; it was an inquisition', and by Sir Michael O'Dwyer's observation, after he had concluded his own evidence, 'I was treated worse than a criminal'. Other witnesses, he said, were treated with less consideration than if they had been prisoners in the dock.

Dyer did face one handicap, as Mr Colvin says, for he depended for his papers on Captain Briggs and he was greatly disturbed by the news that the man was ill and could not come. 'Not only was he anxious for the safety of his friend', remarks Mr Colvin, 'but he was disabled at the outset in the preparation of his case.'

Caution is suggested by Mr Colvin as to the record of the evidence spoken by Dyer, and by Sir Michael O'Dwyer, who, he says, demanded a copy of what he had said and found it so full of mistakes that, after correcting a few pages, he sent it back as hopeless, an experience shared by Commissioner Kitchin, who said in 1924 that the shorthand notes taken gave only a general indication of what the witness said, while 'sometimes the remarks of members of the Committee were reported as being the evidence of witnesses'. General Dyer, says Mr Colvin, could not take the precaution adopted by the ex-Lieutenant-Governor of the Punjab, as 'he was not allowed to see the evidence', and he annotated a copy of the Committee's Report in his own hand, in several places disclaiming the quotations attributed to him. For example, Mr Colvin points out, where Dyer is represented as saying 'I have made up my mind that I would do all men to death if they were going to continue the meeting', he had written 'I emphatically deny this', and Mr Colvin points out that Dyer's denial has probability to support it, 'since it is difficult to imagine any Englishman using such a phrase as "do all men to death", although it is easy to suppose an Indian *babu* putting such words into his mouth'. Against the words, 'Strike terror throughout the Punjab', which he is recorded as saying, Dyer had written, 'No. I do not admit this', and Colvin observes that, 'On reading over General Dyer's evidence, I have found remarks so extraordinary that I consider they could not have been made by the witness'. Puzzled by these and other remarks hardly less preposterous, Colvin took the precaution of seeing Mr Watson, who reported the case for *The Pioneer*: 'He told me that the Committee had got itself into such a mess over the report of the evidence that he had been called into help, and what was finally printed was a mixture of his notes and the official report patched up together'.

'These things being so, it would be manifestly unfair to judge General Dyer on the record of his spoken evidence', declares his biographer, who observes: 'After all, it is not by what he said but by what he did that he should be judged.' Sir George Barrow, who heard the evidence, on the contrary, states, 'There is no doubt that Dyer uttered the words as reported', and he was so struck by his remark about 'doing all men to death' that it stuck in his memory.

Bearing these objections in mind, we can consider what Dyer said, or is reported to have said, in evidence.

Under military law, he told Lord Hunter, it was justifiable to fire on a crowd which had been warned not to collect. He had no doubt, he said, that the crowd knew of his order, but he was forced to admit that his proclamation had not been read in all parts of the city. It did not occur to him there was a risk that some of those present might not have been aware of his order. It had not been obeyed, martial law had been flouted, and it was his duty to disperse the assembly by fire. He had made up his mind that if his orders were not obeyed he would fire immediately. Asked what his objects were, Dyer said he was going to fire until the crowd dispersed, and he fired until they dispersed. They started to disperse at once but he went on firing. It was possible, he thought, that he might have dispersed them without firing. If he had not dispersed the crowd, he said, they would have laughed at him. The rioters were trying to isolate him. The riots were part of a widespread movement. He looked upon these people as rebels, he said, and he considered it his duty to fire and fire well.

It was in answer to Mr Justice Rankin that Dyer made the extraordinary, and perhaps inaccurately recorded, statement that he had made up his mind to 'do all men to death' if they were going to continue the meeting. He thought, he said, it was a sign of rebellion that the crowd had refused to obey his order, and he had looked at the position in Amritsar in the light of the Punjab as a whole. 'I had to do something very strong', he stated, an answer which brought the suggestion he had resorted to 'Frightfulness'. 'No, I don't think so', replied Dyer.

So far Dyer had answered the questions put to him with reasonable caution, but now he allowed himself to be drawn into an indiscreet answer to a hypothetical question posed by Sir C. H. Setalvad, which he could have parried easily by stating that the question did not arise as the event contemplated had not occurred. The Indian lawyer leaned forward:

'You took two armoured cars with you?'
'Yes.'
'Those cars had machine guns?'
'Yes.'
'And when you took them you meant to use the machine guns against the crowd, did you?'
'If necessary. If the necessity arose, and I was attacked, or anything else like that, I presume I would have used them.'
'When you arrived there you were not able to take the armoured cars in because the passage was too narrow?'
'Yes.'
'Supposing the passage was sufficient to allow the armoured cars to go in, would you have opened fire with the machine guns?'
'I think probably yes.'
'In that case the casualties would have been very much higher?'
'Yes.'
'And you did not open fire with the machine guns simply by the accident of the armoured cars not being able to get in?'
'I have answered you. I have said that if they had been there the probability is that I would have opened fire with them.'
'With the machine guns straight?'

'With the machine guns.'

Having extracted this indiscreet and unnecessary admission from the witness, the examiner pushed home the advantage: 'I take it that your idea in taking that action was to strike terror not only in Amritsar but throughout the Punjab?' Setalvad suggested. 'Call it what you like. I was going to punish them, and make a wide impression', replied Dyer. He wanted to reduce the *morale* of the rebels, he said. Asked if he thought the British *Raj* was in danger, Dyer answered, 'No, the British *Raj* is a mighty thing'. His action was justified in saving lives and property, to prevent the mutiny spreading, he said. The inexorable examiner went on:

'Did it occur to you that by adopting this method of "frightfulness"—excuse the term—you were really doing a great disservice to the British *Raj* by driving discontent deep?'

'No, it only struck me that at the time it was my duty to do this and that it was a horrible duty. I did not like the idea of doing it but I also realized that it was the only means of saving life and that any reasonable man with justice in his mind would realize that I had done the right thing; and it was a merciful though horrible act and they ought to be thankful to me for doing it.'

He thought, said Dyer, it would be doing a jolly lot of good and they would realize that they were not to be wicked.

Dyer was forced to admit that he had directed the firing on people lying on the ground and that he had made no attempt to relieve the wounded. They could have applied for help, he said, but they did not do so because they would have been taken into custody for being in the assembly. 'I was ready to help them if they applied', he stated, a remark which did little to soften the blow.

Major-General Sir George Barrow tried to help Dyer to correct the bad impression his answers to the Indian had given by providing him with the opportunity to confirm that he had been instructed to take such measures as he considered necessary to restore order, and that, in view of the very serious situation, he had the right to anticipate the proclamation of martial law. In reference to the Jallianwala Bagh incident, General Barrow pointed out that Dyer presumably knew that 'an unlawful assembly may be dispersed even by force, if necessary, even though it had not actually resorted to acts of violence'. Dyer said he knew that.

General Barrow was not content to leave it at that. In his last question he gave Dyer even further opportunity to justify himself:

'Then you referred once to the seriousness of the situation and said that unless one is faced with a situation of that sort, it is difficult to realize what it means?'
'Yes, Sir.'
'That is, the necessity for prompt action was so essential that there was no time for further reflection?'
'Yes, Sir.'
'And you yourself were so much occupied with the various questions which were brought before you that you had no time to sit down and consider from every point of view what the possible consequences of your action might be?'
'That is true.'
'And also perhaps you will agree with me that when one is faced with such a situation, it creates quite a different impression on one's mind to what it will when you are simply reading about it?'
'Quite true, Sir.'

Something had been retrieved, but Dyer still had to face the questions of another Indian inquisitor, this time Pandit Jayat Narayan, and to his probing question he was forced to admit that no act of lawlessness had been committed by the mob in Amritsar after the 10th, his answer implying that the rebellious mob he had fired upon had shown no further evidence of rioting after that date. Dyer emphasized that he had not made up his mind to fire only because of what had happened in Amritsar.

It was put to Dyer by Mr Herbert, the Government Advocate, that bullet marks on the second and third storeys of buildings surrounding the Bagh suggested he had ordered his soldiers to fire high. 'Certainly not. I never gave such an order. I know what orders I gave. I directed the fire personally. I never gave any order for overhead firing. Absolutely none', stated the witness, vehemently rejecting the implication that he might have fired warning shots at first.

To Mr Herbert's series of questions relating to the possibility that, as Dyer had said the firing was necessary in view of the general situation in the Punjab, he would have fired whether or not he had issued a proclamation, and the effect would have been the same, Dyer replied that it was difficult to say. 'I wanted to punish the naughty boy', he said, adding that 'It would be difficult to say what would be the effect of punishing a boy who is not naughty'. He would have been justified in firing even if he had not made a proclamation, he declared. The men who came to the Bagh, he thought, 'had hostile feelings towards the British *Raj*'. He did not believe they were honest people.

Turning to the administration of martial law in Amritsar, Mr Herbert suggested: 'Have not some of the orders promulgated by you a family likeness to similar orders promulgated (by the Germans) in Belgium? For instance, the order about salaaming and the curfew order?' 'In my mind it had nothing to do with Belgium', Dyer curtly replied.

Pandit Jayat Narayan asked Dyer how he expected people to relieve the wounded and remove the dead in the Bagh while the curfew order was in force? Dyer stated that the curfew order was modified for that purpose, but he admitted that the people had not been so informed. 'I allowed them to do so, that was enough', he said. To further questions addressed to him about the administration of martial law in Amritsar, he complained, 'It is not fair to ask me what happens so long ago. I cannot answer you straight. I don't remember.' To the question as to whether there was any evidence to show that there had been an organized conspiracy, Dyer answered: 'From what happened at Amritsar and elsewhere, I formed the opinion there was a widespread conspiracy'. Asked 'Now when you reached the Jallianwala Bagh, there was no apprehension of your being attacked, as the soldiers were there, or was there a possibility?' he replied, 'There was certainly a possibility'.

Finally, Dyer was subjected to a series of questions by Sardar Sahibzada Sultan Ahmed Khan, who directed his first questions to Dyer's assumption of authority in Amritsar. It was his duty to take matters in hand, Dyer stated, as Commanding Officer. In such an extreme case it was his duty to assume responsibility. Invited to state what were the conditions which constituted an extreme case, Dyer replied: 'Well, in the case of a rebellion, which I honestly thought was a rebellion, I would chance it and take the responsibility. I do not mean that I would be right in every case, but it would be my duty to take the responsibility, and if I was wrong I would suffer.' Asked what constituted rebellion, he replied, 'I should think that if civil law had ceased then a rebellion is on'. In his opinion, that constituted rebellion, he said. In that case he would assume responsibility and 'run the risk'. When he arrived in Amritsar, he knew what had happened there and what was happening elsewhere. What was happening in Amritsar was part of a rebellion, of an organized movement, he believed. Asked if he 'inferred' there was a rebellion, Dyer replied, 'Yes, it looked like it'.

It looked like an organized movement, he said, but he agreed he had no proof. These happenings everywhere might be a coincidence, he agreed, but in his opinion, he said, 'it certainly looked like an organized rebellion'. He did not remember, he said, whether the Deputy Commissioner had told him or not whether there was a branch of such an organization in Amritsar, and he agreed it would have been a good thing if he had issued a proclamation to the effect that he had assumed supreme authority. 'If I had thought a little faster and had a little more time, I think I would have issued such a proclamation', he stated. 'This is the first rebellion I have had to deal with', he pointed out, adding, 'and hereafter, though I hope I will not have to deal with another, I may deal with it differently.'

A few more questions and answers and Dyer's examination was finished. The ordeal was over. His opportunity to justify himself publicly was done. He had been tried and, though he did not yet know it, condemned. The fatal questions had been posed; the fatal answers given. Replies which, truthful or inaccurate, would present Dyer to his fellow countrymen, who now learned about the extent of the firing in the Jallianwala Bagh for the first time, either as the hero who had saved the Punjab, and perhaps all India, or as the inhuman monster who had shot down an unarmed and unresisting crowd, people who were trying to escape.

When Dyer came out of the Committee room, General Beynon asked him, 'Why did you say you went down with the intention of firing?' Dyer answered, 'Of course I intended to fire, if necessary'. 'That is not the impression you have given the Committee', Beynon told him.

Dyer left the Committee hearing, which he was later to criticize as 'irregular and prejudicial', suspecting, we may believe, that the feeling of its members had been against him, for Mr Watson of *The Pioneer* told Mr Colvin, who asked if Dyer had lost his temper, 'On the contrary, he seemed only like a man very weary, who gave up trying to put his case when he saw it was hopeless'.

Dyer had made a number of damaging admissions. He agreed he could have dispersed the mob without firing. But they would have laughed at him, made him feel a fool. He might have used his machine guns, if he could have got them in. His proclamation might not have been heard by everyone. It was not sufficiently emphatic. He had fired without warning and he continued to fire for ten minutes while the crowd was trying to disperse. He fired to teach a lesson, to strike terror, to create a widespread effect. He made no suggestion that there was any danger to his force; no hint that he thought that the crowd was gathering for a rush. The firing was not forced on him; he did it deliberately and intentionally. That was his explanation.

On concluding his evidence, Dyer returned to Jullundur 'astonished', says Mr Colvin, 'at the reports of what he was alleged to have said which appeared in the newspapers'. His journey from Lahore by train provides us with a brief glimpse of Dyer's alleged demeanour at this time, for Mr Nehru, then aged thirty, recalls in his autobiography:

'Towards the end of that year (1919) I travelled from Amritsar to Delhi by the night train. The compartment I entered was almost full and the berths, except the upper one, were occupied by sleeping passengers. I took the vacant upper berth. In the morning I discovered that all my fellow passengers were military officers. They conversed with each other in loud voices which I could not help overhearing. One of them was holding forth in an aggressive and triumphant tone and soon I discovered that he was Dyer, the hero of the Jallianwala Bagh, and he was describing his Amritsar experiences. He pointed out how he had the whole town at his mercy and he felt like reducing the rebellious city to a heap of ashes, but he took pity on it and refrained. He was evidently coming back from Lahore after giving his evidence before the Hunter Committee of Enquiry. I was greatly shocked to hear his conversation and to observe his callous manner. He descended at Delhi station in pyjamas with bright pink stripes, and a dressing gown.'

But perhaps Mr Nehru was a prejudiced observer.

XII

CENSURE

Back at Jullundur once again, and distressed by the news of his wife's illness and Captain Briggs's death, Dyer fell ill with jaundice and gout, and his heart became affected. He was fifty-five years of age. Feeling himself unable to do justice to his work, he applied for six months' leave in England, receiving the curt answer that the Commander-in-Chief 'is unable to sanction leave. If General Dyer wishes to proceed home, it will be necessary for him to vacate his appointment.' But on the same day, January 30, 1920, he received a further message which took the sting from the earlier one. It stated: '(1) His Excellency the Commander-in-Chief approves of Brigadier-General R. E. H. Dyer officiating in Command of the 2nd Division *vice* Major-General Sir Charles Dobell, appointed to exercise command Northern Command pending further orders, and (2) Inform me of the next senior officer who will officiate in command of the 5th Brigade *vice* General Dyer'.

At the darkest moment Dyer had been raised from the command of a Brigade to the command of a Division, 'obviously a very important step in promotion', observes Mr Colvin, which in the ordinary course of promotion carried the rank of Major-General and probably a knighthood. The Commander-in-Chief's decision, taken two months after Dyer had given evidence before the Hunter Committee, to put him in charge of a Division, was taken subsequently by Dyer's supporters to show that the Army High Command supported him, but were then persuaded or frightened into turning their backs on him. Sir George Barrow sets out in his vindication of the Commander-in-Chief to correct this misconception. Dyer, he says, was given temporary command of a Division, during a vacancy. He was not eligible to command a Division and it was not intended that he should hold permanent command. In fact, Dyer's 'promotion' was short-lived, for on February 14th he received a further message which told him that the Commander-in-Chief 'approves Brigadier-General Caulfield continuing in command 2nd Division until Major-General Sheppard takes over. In view of the above,

Brigadier-General Dyer will not now take up Command of the Division on his return from leave.'

What had happened between January 30th and February 14th? Something must have caused Sir Charles Monro to change his mind. Not the Report of the Hunter Committee, which was not handed to the Government of India until March 8th, thinks Mr Colwin, who claims that Monro beat a precipitate retreat before the challenge of Babu Kamini Kumar Chanda, a member of the Legislative Council, who put down the embarrassing question, 'Is it a fact that General Dyer received promotion after the firing in the Jallianwala Bagh?' 'The answer is in the negative', replied the Commander-in-Chief. Sir Michael O'Dwyer has two explanations to offer. 'The question arises—Why and when did those high authorities change their minds?' He explained it thus:

'The Government of India—of which the Commander-in-Chief is a member—were becoming alarmed by the spurious agitation worked up over the Punjab "atrocities", were doubtless being pressed by Mr Montagu to make any concessions that would secure a "calm atmosphere" for the Reforms, and adopted the usual, but ineffective, method of throwing some of their servants to the wolves.'

Secondly, Sir Michael O'Dwyer suggests that portions of the evidence given by Dyer, whom he calls a 'blunt, honest soldier', under the stress of hostile cross-examination, and quoted in the newspapers, made it appear that he had deliberately shot down hundreds of innocent people when he could have dispersed the crowd with a wave of his hand. The outcry in the press against Dyer, says O'Dwyer, was due to ignorance; but 'it was not unnatural', for the Government of India and the India Office, for reasons best known to themselves, 'had never put the press and public at home in possession of the full facts of the 1919 outbreaks, and in particular had issued only the most meagre and misleading summaries of my own and Dyer's reports of April 14th on the firing at Amritsar on April 13th'. Neither he nor Dyer were able, he states, to quote from confidential papers in explanation of their actions, until he himself was allowed, 'with great reluctance and only after my repeated applications', to produce *some* of them in his action in the case of O'Dwyer v. Nair.

Summing up his two explanations, O'Dwyer goes on to say:

'Anyhow, in deference either to the clamour of the extremists in India who were loudly demanding Dyer's prosecution and downfall, as well as my impeachment, or to the outcry of the uninformed press at home, the authorities in India and here decided that it was no longer expedient to support Dyer's actions. On the receipt of the Hunter Committee's Report—the conclusions of which were, as regards Dyer, based on unverified statements and incomplete investigation of the character of the meeting fired upon—they professed to find enough to justify them, a year after the event, in repudiating the action which they had hitherto approved; action which was undoubtedly justified by the local conditions at Amritsar, which undoubtedly saved the Punjab and Northern India from a most serious rebellion, and thus marred the opportunity of successful foreign invasion for which the Afghans and the Frontier tribes were eagerly waiting.'

The conduct of the Army Command, especially in view of the Vice-Regal Resolution of April 14, 1919, promising full countenance and support to officers engaged in suppressing the rebellion, seemed to them harsh and unjust, says O'Dwyer, who continues, 'I felt that even if his own Chiefs deserted him, it was my duty, having been the indirect cause of his having to deal with the Amritsar situation, to do all I could to explain the circumstances and to vindicate his action'. The steps Sir Michael O'Dwyer took to achieve this will appear in due course.

Two significant points emerge from this sudden *volte face* by the Army High Command. Two months after he had publicly explained his reasons for firing in the Jallianwala Bagh, the Army High Command had sufficient confidence in Dyer to raise him to the temporary command of a division. Then, within a few days, it changed its mind. Some very weighty consideration must have arisen to stop the Army from doing what it apparently wanted to do, to exonerate and vindicate Dyer officially, and to show the politicians that the Army stood behind him. What went wrong with the scheme? Why did the Army suddenly get cold feet? The High Command may have been given a hint of the Hunter Committee's conclusions, a reasonable possibility, for rumours of such things leak out. Rather than share Dyer's condemnation, by inference, it dropped him like a hot cake, a reasonable presumption, for that is what usually happens in such cases.

Now Dyer stood alone, the stricken member of the pack, deserted by its mates.

He lay in the British Hospital at Jullundur in great pain and misery of mind, awaiting the next move. He was not kept long in suspense. On March 5th came a telegram addressed to the Commander of the 2nd Division:

'Brigadier-General Dyer at present on sick leave Jullundur should be directed to proceed to Delhi on March 9th and report to me his presence will be required in Delhi for some days.'

The telegram was signed 'Commander-in-Chief'.

The medical officer at the hospital refused to allow Dyer to travel, and on March 18th a second telegram arrived, stating 'General Dyer to proceed to Delhi on 22nd. Report to Military Secretary at 10.30 a.m. on Tuesday 23rd.' The medical officer was still adamant that his patient was unfit to travel, but Dyer was taken from his bed and put on a train for Delhi under the care of an army doctor. On the day named, he presented himself for his audience with the Commander-in-Chief. Sir Havelock Hudson met him in the ante-room. He told Dyer of the Hunter Comittee's censure and that he was to be deprived of his command. When Dyer protested that, as he had never been tried, he should not be condemned, the Adjutant-General stated the matter had been decided and it remained only for Dyer to see Sir Charles Monro. 'The chief', he told him, 'is very much upset. I am sure you will not say anything to distress His Excellency.' 'No,' replied Dyer, 'the last thing I should wish to do would be to distress His Excellency.' Ushered into Monro's presence, Dyer heard his sentence. He said nothing and next day he returned to hospital at Jullundur. Invited at the libel trial in 1924 to say whether he thought Dyer's action was justified, Monro said he thought he acted with a 'little precipitation'.

The Hunter Committee, whose Report the Government of India sent to the Secretary of State in London on May 3rd, adversely criticized Dyer on two grounds, as the Government's accompanying despatch explained. He opened fire without warning, and he went on firing after the crowd had begun to disperse. It remarked that he did not suggest the existence of an emergency justifying his decision to open fire on the crowd without warning, and he said his mind was made up that, if his orders were not obeyed, he was going to fire at once. In continuing to fire as long as he did, even after the crowd had begun to disperse, he had committed a grave error. His intention to create a moral effect was a mistaken conception of his duty. The Committee, the despatch explained, did not accept the view that by his action Dyer saved the situation in the Punjab and averted a rebellion on a scale similar to the Mutiny.

The Government stated the views of the minority members of the Committee, who, it observed, found that the notice prohibiting the meeting was not adequately published, and who criticized General Dyer severely, '(1) for suggesting that he would have made use of machine guns if they could have been brought into action, (2) for opening fire without warning and continuing after the crowd had begun to disperse until his ammunition was spent, (3) for firing not merely to disperse the crowd but to punish it and to produce a moral effect in the Punjab, and (4) for assuming that the crowd before him consisted of the persons guilty of the outrages on the 10th'.

Continuing its digest of the Committee's Minority Report, which was signed by the three Indian members, Setalvad, Narayan and Ahmed Khan, the Government stated:

'They do not agree with the majority that it was probable that the crowd could not have been dispersed without firing, citing General Dyer himself in support of their opinion; and they describe his action as inhuman and un-British and as having caused great disservice to British rule in India. They attribute his conduct to a fixed idea that India must be ruled by force and they condemn his action in not taking steps for the removal of the dead and the care of the wounded.'

The Government despatch went on to say:

'The difference in the measure of condemnation of General Dyer by the Majority and the Minority, and the attention which has been directed to the events at the Jallianwala Bagh both in England and in India, necessitates a careful examination by the Government of the extent to which General Dyer should be held blameworthy. Looking to the specific findings on which the condemnation of his action is based, we consider that the orders prohibiting assemblies should have been promulgated more widely and in particular that notices might have been posted up at Jallianwala Bagh, which had become a favourite assembly for political meetings. We think also that notice might have been given at the Baiskhi fair where many people from villages in the vicinity had collected. At the same time it is the case that the proclamation was made by beat of drum in the presence of General Dyer himself, and notices were published at nineteen places in the city; it cannot therefore be doubted that most of the residents of Amritsar present at the meeting were aware of the orders and collected in defiance of them.'

The Government of India stated that it agreed with the Committee that General Dyer should have given warning to the crowd before opening fire. Its despatch continued:

'It is true that he had only a small force with him and that in view of this circumstance and the previous excesses of the forces disorder it is most improbable that an excited and defiant mob would have dispersed on a mere warning, but those ignorant of the order, including visitors who had come to visit the Baiskhi fair, and indeed others would have had an opportunity of leaving the assembly if reasonable notice had been given to them. The Government of India agree that there was not such an emergency existing as to render this precaution impossible.'

General Dyer's action in continuing to fire on the crowd after it had begun to disperse was, the Government of India stated, 'indefensible', and it declared though it was probable that General Dyer's action so intimidated the lawless elements of Amritsar and the neighbouring districts as to prevent further manifestations of disorder, that was no justification for him continuing to fire, 'which greatly exceeded the necessity of the occasion'. The dispersal of the crowd was indeed a matter of vital importance, stated the despatch, but it said that General Dyer's action 'has undoubtedly left behind bitterness of feeling which will take a long time to pass away'.

In the words of the despatch, General Dyer 'was no doubt faced with a position of great difficulty; he was apprehensive of Amritsar being isolated and he had before him the danger of allowing mob rule to continue after the terrible events of the 10th'. Summing up, the Government of India stated:

'Giving all due weight to these considerations, the deliberate conclusion at which we have arrived is that General Dyer exceeded the reasonable requirements of the case and showed a misconception of his duty which resulted in a lamentable and unnecessary loss of life.'

Although constrained to this decision, stated the despatch, the

Government was convinced that General Dyer acted honestly in the belief that he was doing what was right and that, in the result, his action checked the spread of the disturbances to an extent difficult to estimate. 'That was the opinion of many intelligent observers in the Punjab', the Government said. It expressed its great regret that no action was taken to remove the dead and aid the wounded, and, in respect of the minority members' rebuke of Sir Michael O'Dwyer for expressing approval of Dyer's action, it had, it said, little to add except to express the opinion that he would have acted more wisely if, before expressing any approval, he had taken steps to ascertain the facts and circumstances of the firing more fully.

Finally, in discussing the conduct of various officers criticized by the Committee, the Government's despatch stated that 'the case of General Dyer calls for separate mention', and it said it had given most anxious consideration to his action at the Jallianwala Bagh. It continued: 'We are satisfied that it was *bona fide* and dictated by a stern though misconceived sense of duty', and it observed that he had made no attempt to minimize his responsibility for the tragedy or 'even to put a favourable complexion on his action or purpose'. The only justification that could be pleaded for his conduct, the Government of India said, was that of military necessity. In circumstances such as those with which he was confronted, it pointed out, 'an officer must act honestly and vigorously, but with as much humanity as the case will permit'. It recognized, the Government stated, that in the face of a great crisis an officer might be thrown temporarily off the balance of his judgment and that allowance must be made on that account, and it recognized further that, however injurious in its ultimate effect General Dyer's action might have been, it resulted in an immediate discouragement of the forces of disorder. Nor, said the Government, had it overlooked its own Resolution which promised full countenance and support to officers engaged in the onerous duty of suppressing disorder. Nevertheless, after carefully weighing all these factors, it could arrive at no other conclusion than that, at the Jallianwala Bagh, General Dyer acted beyond the necessity of the case, beyond what any reasonable man could have thought to be necessary, and that he did not act with as much humanity as the case permitted. 'It is with pain that we arrive at this conclusion', the Government found, 'for we are not forgetful of General Dyer's distinguished record as a soldier or of his gallant relief of the Garrison of Thal during the recent Afghan War'. It must, however, direct that the judgment pronounced be communicated to the Commander-in-Chief with the request that he take appropriate action.

The Hunter Committee had censured him; that Dyer now knew. The Government of India was likely to condemn him; that Dyer must have expected.

The Committee's report also criticized other officials, and it considered the cause of the disturbances and their nature, matters which have a bearing on our assessment of Dyer's action for, like Sir Michael O'Dwyer, he claimed that they were part of a centrally organized conspiracy, a rebellion, a revolt against British rule, which, if true, provided some justification for the drastic action he took on April 13th.

The Hunter Committee upheld all the cases of firing, at Delhi, Ahmedabad, Vizamgam, Lahore, Kasur, Gujrianwala and at Amritsar on the 10th, except the firing in the Jallianwala Bagh, and in support of its opinion that the disorders were more or less spontaneous it quoted the testimony of the Deputy Inspector-General of Police in the Punjab, who had made a special investigation of their causes, 'that behind and beneath the disturbances there was no organization as could not have been seen by anyone following political development in India during the last few years'. The disorders, for which the agitation against the Rowlatt Acts was largely responsible, were not, the Committee found, 'the result of a prearranged conspiracy to overthrow the British Government in India by force', but it realized that 'it was difficult and probably unsafe for the Government not to assume that the outbreak was not the result of a definite organization'. The majority members declared that the disorders were the result of a movement which started in rioting, became a rebellion, and might have become a revolution, but the minority members found that an exaggeration, and they gave their view that the outbreak resulted from an outburst of anti-British feeling brought on by sudden mob-frenzy. The civil authorities persuaded themselves that open rebellion had broken out and they acted accordingly. The disorders, declared the minority, did not amount to a rebellion.

Dealing with the outbreak at Amritsar on the 10th, the majority members thought that the firing at the bridge was in no sense the cause of the excesses of the mob. The minority believed that, though the excesses were inexcusable, the mob had no previous intention to commit excesses, but that after the firing the people lost their heads and were seized with mad frenzy. The subsequent handing over of control to the military by the civil authorities, in such terms as to suggest they did not intend to exercise supervision or guidance, was regretted by the Government of India who observed that, as a result, it placed the military commander in a position of great difficulty and imposed on him a responsibility which, in the opinion of the Government, should have continued to be shared by the civil authorities. Considering the measures taken to suppress the disorders in the Punjab, the Government of India found that Sir Michael O'Dwyer 'acted with decision and vigour at a time of great danger', and it said that he was largely responsible for quelling a dangerous rising 'which might have had widespread and disastrous effects on the rest of India'.

Dyer, the Committee considered, had quelled the disorders, which were no more than spontaneous outbursts resulting from misrepresentation of the Rowlatt Acts and the consequent agitation. He had neither 'saved' the Punjab nor 'prevented' another Mutiny. It also severely criticized his crawling order and certain measures taken by other officers during the administration of martial law, in particular, General Campbell's 'salaaming order', Colonel Johnson's 'roll call' of students, the flogging of boys because they happened to be big, the flogging of the innocent village headman, the flogging of members of the wedding party, Captain Doveton's 'fancy' punishments and floggings in public. The minority members found themselves unable to uphold Captain Carberry's bombings and machine-gunnings at Gujrianwala. The majority upheld, and the minority criticized, the introduction of martial law, and in combination they found that its administration had been 'marred in particular instances by a measure of power, by irregularities, and by injudicious and irresponsible acts', and they considered these defects to be due to lack of proper instructions, ignorance of local conditions and lack of guidance rather than from a deliberate misuse of power. In general, officers had acted with admirable restraint.

The Indian National Congress Sub-Committee, which had been taking evidence independently, published its report on February 20, 1920, finding that the Jallianwala Bagh massacre was 'a calculated piece of inhumanity towards utterly innocent and unarmed men, including children, and unparalleled for its ferocity in the history of modern British administration'. It demanded the impeachment of Dyer and of other officials, and the recall of the Viceroy.

This report was published in India a month before the Commander-in-Chief informed Dyer that his services were no longer required.

On the day after his return to Jullundur, following his audience with Sir Charles Monro, Dyer received a letter from the Commander-in-Chief informing him, 'Your application for permission to resign your appointment should be made as soon as possible, and forwarded through the proper channels, for disposal under the Chief's orders. The subsequent orders granting you permission will state what—if any, war or other leave will be admitted to you.' As a result, on March 27th, Dyer wrote to his immediate superior, the General commanding the 2nd Division: 'Sir, I have the honour to state that during my recent visit to Delhi, the Adjutant-General in India informed me that, owing to the opinion expressed by the Hunter Committee regarding my action in Amritsar during April 1919, it was necessary for me to resign my appointment as Brigadier-General commanding the 5th Infantry Brigade. Accordingly I hereby ask that I be relieved of that appointment.'

Dyer set about winding up his affairs in India, which necessitated visits to Jamrud and Rayalpindi, permission for him to travel to these places being rather grudgingly accorded by the Commander-in-Chief, if Mr Colvin is to be believed. Dyer, he says, was subjected to several contradictory and extraordinary orders which suggests 'that the Commander-in-Chief, in his sudden and belated access of moral indignation at the events of Amritsar, thought it necessary to be discourteous to General Dyer', and he considers it probable 'that the Higher Command feared a demonstration in his favour among the troops at the great military centre at Rawalpindi, a thing General Dyer would have disliked no less'.

Dyer and his wife, when they drove to the railway station at Jullundur at night to entrain for Bombay, found its approaches lit by flares placed on both sides of the road and under them Sepoys of all the Indian regiments standing at the salute. Mr Colvin says: 'There was, besides, a great guard of honour of all the non-commissioned officers at the railway station itself. This demonstration had been arranged by the men and the N.C.O's upon their own initiative without any authority from their own officers; but the officers came down with their wives, to bid the

General farewell at the station which was packed with a great concourse of people.' 'General Dyer was very shy of such demonstrations', says his biographer, who adds, 'but this had so much in it both spontaneity and feeling that it touched and comforted him. He left Jullundur with the cheers of his comrades ringing in his ears.'

Dyer sailed for England, arriving at Southampton on May 2nd. He could not dispute the right of the Commander-in-Chief, India, to relieve him of his command, Mr Colvin observes, but Dyer had reason to believe that he was to be dismissed from the Army. 'He had submitted to discipline', but 'he could not submit to disgrace.'

XIII

CONTROVERSY

Dyer had not yet seen the Hunter Report. He knew only that it had censured him. His command in India had been taken from him; his career was jeopardized, his future threatened. He believed that he had acted rightly, that by his action he had saved the Punjab. At the Hunter Committee hearing he had not been given a fair opportunity to present his case. That could now be remedied. Within a week of his arrival in London, he wrote to the Military Secretary at the India Office, requesting that his action at Amritsar should be considered by the Army Council, and he asked that he should be permitted to present his case personally, attended, if necessary, by a legal adviser.

How Dyer's application was dealt with is explained by Field-Marshal Sir Henry Wilson, the Chief of the Imperial General Staff, whose 'unhibited diary', published in 1927, caused 'such anguish', in the words of Barbara Tuchman (*August 1914-1962*).

The Dyer case had been under consideration by the Cabinet for some months when Mr Winston Churchill, Secretary of State for War, brought it up at a meeting of the Army Council on May 14th. According to Sir Henry Wilson, 'Winston made a long speech, prejudicing the case and in effect saying that the Cabinet, and he, had decided to throw out Dyer, but that it was advisable for the Army Council to agree'. Wilson stated he had not had time to read the papers and he was unable to express an opinion. The other military members took the same stand, though Churchill said the matter was pressing. At the next meeting, a week later, says Wilson, 'Winston tried again to rush a decision to remove Dyer from the Army', but the military members insisted he be allowed to state his case. This decision did not suit Mr Churchill who, records Wilson, sent for him and said, 'he was much upset by this "pistol at his head by the military members", and that in future he would have to take precautions against these "ambushes".'

Mr Churchill, according to Wilson, brought the matter up again at the next Army Council meeting, stating that the Cabinet had decided to remove Dyer. The military members pointed out that they had not had time to consider the case. Churchill tried to argue, but 'the more he argued, the deeper I put him in the "muckheap" ', says Wilson. Churchill gave it up at last, agreeing that nothing should be done until they had had another meeting.

At this stage of the proceedings the Army Council received a letter from Dyer asking to be allowed to rebut the Hunter Report. It was agreed to send him a copy of the report, which he had not seen, and invite his answer. Though Churchill, when he was told, agreed this procedure was reasonable, he again informed Wilson that the Cabinet was unanimous in their determination to fling Dyer out. They would not hear of leaving him on full pay, and he hinted, says Wilson, of the difficulties which would arise if the military members differed from the Cabinet. According to Wilson, Churchill told him on June 9th, that Dyer's statement was not 'to go out', by which he presumably meant 'published', until after the debate in the House of Commons, a motion for which had already been tabled by Dyer's supporters, one the discussion of which was postponed until after Dyer had submitted his statement.

These extracts from Sir Henry Wilson's diary have carried us ahead of events. Mr Colvin tells us that, 'When Sir Michael O'Dwyer saw the Hunter Committee's report on his return from India, he applied to Mr Montagu to be allowed to make a statement, not on his own behalf but to explain those circumstances of Amritsar which the Committee had failed to grasp. When his application was refused he applied officially to the Army Council to be heard before they passed orders on Dyer's case. That application also was rejected, and it was never seen by the military members of the Army Council.'

Without hearing O'Dwyer, and before a decision had been reached by the Army Council about Dyer, the Secretary of State for India published the Hunter report on May 27th, and with it a public dispatch addressed to the Government of India.

The principle governing military action in support of civil authority was the use of minimum force, stated Mr Montagu. Dyer, he declared, had acted in complete violation of that principle. It was possible that he would have found it impossible to disperse the crowd effectively without some loss of life, but he made no attempt to ascertain the minimum amount of force he was compelled to employ. The force he did employ was greatly in excess of the amount required. That was not his full error; his proclamation had been read only in a portion of the city, and his failure to give medical assistance to the wounded and dying was an omission from his obvious duty. But the gravest error was his avowed conception of his duty in the circumstances which confronted him. The Government, declared Mr Montagu, repudiated emphatically 'the doctrine upon which Brigadier-General Dyer based his action—action which, to judge from his own statement, might have taken an even more drastic form had he had a large force at his disposal and had a physical accident not prevented him from using his armoured cars'.

The Government, stated the Secretary of State, thought it was possible that the danger in the Punjab was greater than the Hunter Committee thought. Dyer, he pointed out, knew what was taking place in the Punjab, and he was entitled to lay his plans with reference to those conditions. But he was not, Montagu emphasized, 'entitled to select for condign punishment an unarmed crowd, which, when he inflicted their punishment, had committed no act of violence, had made no attempt to oppose him by force, and many members of which must have been unaware that they were disobeying his commands'.

Mr Montagu ended his dispatch to the Government of India with these pregnant words:

'That Brigadier-General Dyer displayed honesty of purpose and unflinching adherence to his conception of his duty cannot for a moment be questioned. But his conception of his duty in the circumstances in which he was placed was so fundamentally at variance with that which His Majesty's Government had a right to expect from and a duty to enforce upon officers who hold His Majesty's commission, that it is impossible to regard him as fitted to remain entrusted with the responsibility which his rank and position impose upon him. You have reported to me that the Commander-in-Chief has directed Brigadier-General Dyer to resign his appointment as Brigade Commander and has informed him that he would receive no further employment in India, and that you have concurred. I approve this decision and the circumstances of the case have been referred to the Army Council.'

The British Government also censured Dyer for his crawling order, and it condemned the actions of other officers during the administration of martial law, who had 'flouted the standards of propriety and humanity'. It did not regard Sir Michael O'Dwyer as immune from blame in his endorsement of Dyer's action, Mr Montagu said, and he paid tribute to his great energy, decision and courage.

The Government's censure of Dyer was made public on May 27th when, for the first time, he saw the judgment on which he had been condemned.

'In publishing these papers before the Army Council had come to its decision, Mr Montague may have calculated on coercing that body', observes Mr Colvin. General Dyer, he points out, was invited by the Army Council to submit his case in writing on June 9th, and this he did on July 3rd, knowing, we can discern from reviews of the Hunter Report and from newspaper editorials and correspondents, that a large section of the British public considered him 'the Saviour of India'. 'Brigadier-General Dyer saved the situation', declared Major-General Sir O'Moore Creak in the *Nineteenth Century*. Whether he had fired too many rounds or not, no one could say who was not on the spot. The anonymous reviewer in the *Fortnightly Review* found it was neither inhuman nor un-British to 'crush an incipient revolution by one sharp stroke'. The ultra-conservative *Morning Post* backed Dyer. It called his treatment an 'ugly farce', and it stated he had been sacrificed to the susceptibilities of native agitators. The Government's censure of Dyer was 'painful to every honest Englishman and absolutely terrifying to Europeans in India'. He had been faced with a 'howling mob'. He had been treated disgracefully. It stressed that the Hunter Committee had failed to get down to any sort of explanation of the origin of the outbreak, and it quoted the views of Sir Verney Lovett, K.C.S.I., who observed, 'never since the Mutiny have mobs simultaneously rioted and committed murder in cities so far apart'. The eruptions of violence had occurred, by a strange coincidence, on one day at points a thousand miles apart. The existence of a conspiracy was unmistakable. But for Dyer the insurrection would have spread like wildfire. In a week the whole Province would have been ablaze. The agitators responsible for the rebellion had turned its suppression into a burning grievance, and the Government had adopted the old device of throwing over those who did their work at the moment of peril. The Indian English language newspapers were no less enthusiastic in Dyer's support, the *Statesman* declaring that the measures taken by him were inevitable in the circumstances, and the *Mirror* saying he had been sacrificed to political exigencies. The Europeans in India strongly upheld

Dyer, stated the President of the European Association in a letter to *The Times*.

During the month of June, Dyer worked hard at his justification, being advised by his solicitors, Messrs. Sharpe and Pritchard, who procured him the assistance of two barristers, Reginald Hills and Austin Jones.

XIV

JUSTIFICATION

Fortified and encouraged by these manifestations of support, Dyer submitted his case to the Army Council in a written Statement, dated July 3, 1920, and entitled 'Disturbances in the Punjab', a document which was printed by His Majesty's Stationery Office as a Command Paper presented to Parliament.

His action was justifiable, he claimed. It was necessary for him to show, he stated, only that he had acted for the best and that he had reasonable ground for his action. He criticized the Hunter Committee's method of investigation, calling it 'irregular and prejudicial', and stating that the procedure of a trial had not been attempted. He had not expected to find himself an accused person, and he was given no opportunity to question other witnesses. Several members of the Committee acted as his prosecutors. He was given no opportunity to correct inaccuracies in the transcript of evidence. As a result he had now seen for the first time, and all at once, charges, evidence and findings. This procedure was not in accordance with the course of justice normally observed, and it was irregular according to both military law and custom.

He was well acquainted with the principle of 'minimum force', he said, and, in his best judgment, he had used at Amritsar no more force than was required by the occasion.

In his testimony to the Hunter Committee, it needs to be recalled, Dyer gave two definite reasons for firing on the crowd, to punish it and to create a widespread impression. In his statement to the Army Council he gave other reasons. Since his return from India he had learned discretion, or had apparently been well advised.

He was aware, he said, of the threatening nature of the Afghan situation, the weakness of the internal military situation and the threat to communications. On his arrival at Amritsar he was confronted with a crisis of the gravest kind. It was beyond civil control, and he found the clear conviction upon the part of the local officials and abundant signs that 'a determined and organized movement was in progress to submerge and destroy all the Europeans on the spot and in the district and to carry the movement throughout the Punjab'. He was confronted, not with a riot, but with open rebellion. The restrained firing on the 10th had produced no effect at all, and the situation was more menacing than ever. He had only a small force at his disposal and the countryside around Amritsar was densely populated with people of an inflammable character. He was left in no doubt, he said, as to the existence of an organized mob with leaders, with a definite purpose of outrage and destruction, and to prove his claim he quoted extracts from the testimony given by Mr Miles Irving who told the Hunter Committee:

'They were working up some kind of mischief which I could not foresee. It struck me that the leaders of the movement were discipling the mob with a view to some concerted form of passive disobedience to authority which would paralyze government.

'My idea was that they intended to avoid any collision with authority that would justify armed intervention and to train the mob to do what they were told.'

Vast supplies of bludgeons were intercepted at the railway, Dyer observed, and he remarked that the Adjutant-General, in his speech on September 19th, had declared that he, Dyer, would have been justified in using military force on the 12th, but he had adopted a policy of patience and conciliation. He hoped, he said, that his proclamation on the 13th would quiet the situation. But it was answered by an immediate challenge. It was rumoured that his action was mere pretence and that he dared not fire. When he learned that the meeting was being held, he knew that the final crisis had come. He knew also, he explained:

'That the assembly was primarily of the same mobs which had murdered and looted and burnt three days previously, and showed their truculence and contempt of the troops during the intervening days, that it was a deliberate challenge to the Government forces, and that if it were not dispersed, and dispersed effectively, with sufficient impression upon the designs and arrogance of the rebels and their followers we should be overwhelmed during the night or the next day by a combination of the city gangs and of the still more formidable multitude from the villages. A crowd from the city of 30,000 had menaced the civil settlement on the 10th. Its audacity in the meantime had grown with its crimes and their immunity. The villages had been brought in, and I had to reckon upon the possibility of the irruption that night of some 30,000 Majha Sikh looters, if the whole movement were not decisively checked.'

He went to the Jallianwala Bagh with his special party, 'none of them at all highly trained men'. There he found a large meeting being addressed by a speaker in violent exhortation, and he reminded the Army Council that the speakers were later convicted of sedition. There were no women or children at the meeting, he stated. His position was an anxious one, as he was liable to be assailed from behind and the extrication of his small force from the city would have been practically impossible, if, after the firing, the rebels had maintained an aggressive spirit. He continued:

'Hesitation, I felt, would be dangerous and futile, and as soon as my fifty riflemen had deployed I ordered fire to be opened. The crowd began to scatter to the various exits. After some firing two groups appeared to be collecting as though to rush us, and on my Brigade-Major calling my attention to this I directed fire specially to the two points in question and dispersed the groups. When 1,650 rounds or thereabouts had been fired, and roughly ten minutes from the time of opening fire, the whole crowd had dispersed, and I was able to lead the body of troops back in security having, as it turned out, established general security in Amritsar and the neighbourhood for everyone. The spirit of the organized mob was effectively broken, and the unrest in the countryside stopped.'

Dealing with the 'connection between Amritsar and the rest of the Punjab', Dyer declared that his action had been the decisive factor in the crushing of the rebellion, and he remarked he could not understand how the crushing of the rebellion, the intimidation of lawless elements, the prevention of further disorder and the checking of the spread of disturbances were not proper objects upon which to employ a military force during a rebellion.

Yet, he stressed, according to the charge against him, these were not proper objects to have endeavoured to secure. How could it be suggested, he asked, that the casualties he inflicted were out of proportion to the result, the suppression of the rebellion? If these were the right objects to pursue, then there was no case against him. The Hunter Committee's criticism of his action implied that his sole right should have been to secure the purely mechanical effect of causing the crowd to move off somewhere else. The fact that it might 'go off full of derision and contempt for my force and burn and loot elsewhere or to surround my troops as they moved out of the city', should not have influenced his action, according to the Hunter Committee.

The mob he faced was the same mob, under the same leaders, which had perpetrated the outrages on the 10th, had been the disturbing force during the subsequent period, and constituted the danger for the future. He had before him in the Jallianwala Bagh not a fortuitous gathering, which at worst had assembled negligently or even recklessly contrary to a proclamation, but a mob that was there with the express intent to challenge Government authority and defy him to take any effective action against it, and to defy him to fire upon it. He knew that it was in substance the same mob that had been in course of organization for some days and had committed the hideous crimes of April 10th, and was the power and authority which for two days had ruled the city in defiance of the Government. In fact, he had the rebel army in front of him.

He knew, so far as human foresight could go, that if he shirked the mob's challenge and did not then and there crush it, it would have succeeded in the design of its leaders. Contempt and derision of Government power would have been complete, and that there would have infallibly followed that night or next morning a general mob movement both from inside and outside Amritsar which would have destroyed all the European population, including women and children and all his troops, and involved in its ruin the law-abiding Indian population as well. He knew that this result would lead to a similar result in numerous places throughout the Punjab.

He knew that on the four occasions when firing took place on the 10th in Amritsar, its effects in preventing disorder and restoring security had been quite ineffective, and that with the small body of troops at his disposal, and the large, determined and defiant assembly before him he could produce no sufficient effect except by continuous firing.

If one dominant motive could be extracted, he said, it was 'the determination to avert from the European women and children and those of the law-abiding Indian community the fate which I was convinced would be theirs, if I did not meet the challenge and produce the required effect to restore order and security'. He was conscious, he said, that it was this motive which gave him the strength of will to carry out his duty.

Summarizing these considerations, Dyer submitted "if my object be admitted to be a proper object, namely, the restoration of order and security, and if I was not confined to the bare mechanical operation of getting the crowd 'to move on', then no evidence or ground is anywhere suggested to show that the force I used was in the least degree excessive.'

Summing up his objects and motives, he claimed:

'(1) That the object which I sought was a right object,
(2) That the force I used was not excessive for the purpose,
(3) That, as the result showed, it did achieve the effect desired, and
(4) That no less force on that occasion would have achieved that effect.'

He believed, he said, that everyone in the crowd knew he had assembled in defiance of the proclamation, and they had revolutionary intent. It would have been futile, he declared, to address the crowd before firing because no further warning would have induced them to disperse. The approach of the troops, which must have been heralded to the crowd, was itself a warning, he observed. The crowd was not as innocent as the Secretary of State made out, he suggested. The idea never entered his head, he said, of firing on an innocent gathering in order to produce an impression. It was not, he stated, an ordinary political meeting composed of non-criminal elements, as the minority members of the Hunter Committee claimed. The whole crowd knew, he was convinced, that they were gathering in defiance of the authorities.

He faced a dense warlike population, inflamed with criminal excesses, and he had only 1,146 troops. If the city mob and the outside villagers had joined hands, 'as assuredly they would have done', the troops and the civil lines would have been taken and communications would have been cut further. He was alive to the situation on the frontier and he knew of attempts to seduce troops. The situation was grave. He had no doubt that he was dealing with no mere local disturbance but with a rebellion, and an essential feature of the conspiracy was the isolation of centres and the cutting of communications to prevent military concentrations. He went on to state:

JUSTIFICATION

'I was conscious of a great offensive movement gathering against me, and knew that to sit still and await its complete mobilization would be fatal. When, therefore, the express challenge by this movement in the shape of the assembly in the Jallianwala Bagh came to me, I knew that a military crisis had come, and that to view the assembly as a mere political gathering, requiring simply to be induced to go away because it was there in breach of an order, was wholly remote from the facts and the necessities of the case. Amritsar was in fact the storm centre of a rebellion. The whole Punjab had its eyes on Amritsar, and the assembly of the crowd that afternoon was for all practical purposes a declaration of war by leaders whose hope and belief was that I should fail to take up the challenge.'

A grave injustice had been done him, he submitted, by the lack of acknowledgement that he was possessed of any feelings of humanity or regard for human life. This combined with clear accusations of Prussian brutality and indifference to innocent suffering had, he claimed, greatly prejudiced his case, which would hardly have arisen if he had been given proper warning of the charges against him. He had neither lost his head, nor acted in any spirit of inhumanity, Dyer protested.

Finally, Dyer summarized his contentions and conclusion. He had said enough, he submitted, to justify his action, and that the circumstances required that he should act as he did. He had acted in good faith and he had reasonable ground for his action. He should, therefore, be finally exonerated from blame. He did not question the right of the Commander-in-Chief not to continue his appointment, if he considered his employment was likely to cause embarrassment, but he submitted there was no case for his censure. The Army Council, he felt confident, would not fail to consider the responsibility which rested upon him and the possible consequences to the Punjab had he failed in energy and determination.

In his statement to the Army Council, there were new reasons which appear to have influenced him, points out Sir George Barrow, 'the situation on the Afghan frontier, the impending murder of British men, woman and children at Amritsar and throughout the Punjab, the organization of the villages and other places for the purpose of committing further atrocities; the ineffectiveness of the firing which had taken place on previous occasions; and the danger to his own force'.

'Surely these were sufficiently weighty causes to be worth imparting to the Hunter Committee. Why was no mention made of them on that occasion?', asks Sir George Barrow, who goes on to say:

'Perhaps Dyer surmised that they would not have carried conviction into the minds of the Hunter Committee or the Government of India. They certainly would not. The more closely one examines them the less convincing do they become. Perhaps when he appeared before the Hunter Committee, Dyer had not formulated them clearly in his own mind, although he had plenty of time to do so, especially as they would have been occupying his thoughts for some time previous to his proceeding to the Jallianwallah Bagh.

'Whatever may have been the reasons which accounted for the reticence he maintained on these points until after his departure from India, they have not been communicated by Dyer or by anyone else. But one thing is evident, namely, either on account of the strain of the situation in which he found himself, or from a temperamental excitability, Dyer's imagination conceived a great deal more than was warranted by the actual facts.'

Sir George Barrow, in his vindication of Sir Charles Monro from the alleged slurs of Dyer's biographer, proceeds to analyze the several reasons given by Dyer:

The organized movement. 'Not only did no one else, qualified to give an opinion on the subject, see any of these signs of a determined and organized movement, but all the available information goes to show that the atrocities which were committed were the unpremeditated deeds of frenzied mobs acting on the spur of the moment under the influence of incontrollable excitement.'

The Afghan invasion. 'A knowledge of the fact that there were certain military activities in Afghanistan which did, as it happened, culminate three weeks later, in a feeble effort at invading India, can hardly be accepted as a contributory cause for opening fire on a recalcitrant crowd in Amritsar. In any case it was not the business of a comparatively junior officer to take this into account, without instructions from higher authority that, owing to a serious military situation elsewhere, extraordinary methods of repression were to be employed against any attempted rising in India. As there was neither a serious military situation nor any signs of an organized conspiracy against established Government, the higher authorities naturally did not issue any such instructions. Dyer went outside his province if he allowed a future possible development on the frontier to influence his actions in Amritsar.'

The defiant mob in the Jallianwallah Bagh was in substance the same mob which had committed the hideous crimes of the 10th. 'It was legitimate for Dyer to assume that some of the persons in the crowd had taken part in the previous outrages, but to say that it was in substance the same crowd was going too far. It would, of course, have been a matter of very great difficulty to collect again into anything like the same crowd, any of those disorganized and fortuitous mobs which had gathered together two days previously.' Sir George Barrow points out also 'we know that one quarter of the crowd was composed of innocent villagers'.

The presumption that there would have been further murders. 'These assumptions are discounted by what has already been said regarding the composition of the crowd. Defiance, sullenness, there may have been, but murder was not in the mind of the crowd assembled in the Jallianwallah Bagh. The mass psychology of a heterogeneous collection of people being what it is, there is no saying what a crowd may or may not do under the influence of demagogic oratory or other cause of excitement. It would be open to Dyer to say that he anticipated certain disastrous results which would follow a failure on his part to disperse the crowd and from not using measures of exceptional severity in order to do so. But Amritsar had been quiet for two whole days before the Jallianwallah crowd assembled. The people of the countryside were peaceful and uninterested; and as to what was likely to occur in other parts of the Punjab, Dyer had not personal cognizance. There was no sort of evidence forthcoming that pointed to the intention or likelihood of a general European massacre at Amritsar and throughout the Punjab. Dyer's confident assertions that he *knew* certain things would *infallibly* happen were not founded on any known facts: he himself produced no facts or information which would bear them out: they were nothing more than creations of his imagination.'

The danger to his small force. 'Dyer has told us that he fired at once and continued to fire in order to produce a moral "widespread effect"; he said he thought it quite possible he could have dispersed the crowd without firing; his reply to a remark made by General Beynon that he did not understand why Dyer had shot so many was that the mob, while endeavouring to escape, was gathering for a rush; he said he feared the mob might try to get round him and assail him from behind. It is impossible to reconcile these statements.' Barrow remarks that Dyer made no suggestion to the Hunter Committee of anything in the demeanour of the crowd which had the appearance of a threat to his own force, and he points out that the danger of his force being assailed from behind was extremely small, especially because of the presence of the two armoured cars equipped with machine-guns. As to the danger of his small force being overwhelmed by a sudden rush, Barrow observes that, whatever the possibility of this, it 'must have passed away long before the ten minutes of its continuation (the firing) had elapsed.' Dyer's apprehensions regarding the safety of his force 'appear to have come as an afterthought', suggests Barrow.

The firing on the 10th ineffective. That was not true, claims Barrow, for it had been completely successful in preventing the mob from reaching the civil lines. There were no further mob excesses and the spirit of rebellion burnt itself out, he says.

These criticisms of Dyer's 'justification' are those of a soldier who was in India at the time of the disorders and who was a member of the Hunter Committee which heard all the evidence. A man who knew what he was talking about.

XV

DECISION

The Army Council's decision on the Dyer case was announced on July 7th in the House of Commons by the Secretary of State for War, Mr Winston Churchill. General Dyer had committed an error of judgment; he was to be retired on half pay with no prospects of future employment.

The Government's decision was not popular in England. Voting strictly on party lines, the House of Commons supported the Government, but the tenor of the debate disclosed considerable Conservative support for Dyer, and 129 Members voted for him. The *Morning Post* started a fund for the 'Saviour of India' and was overwhelmed with contributions, which within a few weeks reached the colossal sum of £26,317. Satisfactory as were these expressions of popular approval, the vote in the Lords carried his vindication even further. Into the Lobby against the Government went 129 Lords; only 86 supported it. Even so, the wave of approval was not done; in 1924 an English Judge expressed the opinion he had acted rightly and had been wrongly punished.

These parliamentary debates did not affect Dyer's position, but they reflect contemporary opinion about this action. The two opposing factions, the politicians who condemned him, and those who declared he had been right to fire on the crowd and had thereby saved India, divided themselves on two main issues. In the official view Dyer had infringed the principle of 'minimum force', wherein an officer must confine himself to a limited and definite object; he fired without warning and he fired too long. It was not the business of a comparatively junior officer to take the wider aspects of the situation into consideration. His declared intention to teach a moral lesson was terrorism, frightfulness, an action described by Mr Churchill as a 'monstrous' event, one that stood 'in singular and sinister isolation'. The pro-Dyer, or anti-Government group, for their motives were clearly mixed, maintained on the other hand that he had been 'broken' for what, at the worst, was a tragic error of judgment. More probably, he had saved the Punjab from worse outrages for the riots were clearly part of a wide-organized conspiracy, a precursor to revolution. He had been condemned without trial. He had been treated shamefully by an ungrateful Government which had promised its servants 'full countenance and support'.

The issue was put to the House of Commons by the Secretary of State for India:

'I will content myself by asking the House one question. If an officer justifies his conduct, no matter how gallant his record is—and everybody knows how gallant General Dyer's record is—by saying that there was no question of undue severity, that if his means had been greater the casualties would have been greater, and that the motive was to teach a moral lesson to the whole of the Punjab, I say without hesitation, and I would ask the Committee to contradict me if I am wrong, because the whole matter turns upon this, that it is the doctrine of terrorism.'

As Secretary of State for War, Mr Churchill justified the Government's action in retiring Dyer. He explained the position:

'The conduct of an officer might be dealt with in three perfectly distinct spheres. He might be removed from his employment, relegated to half-pay and told he had no prospects of re-employment. To do that it was sufficient for a competent superior authority to decide that the interest of the public service would be better served if somebody else was appointed. The officer in question had no redress. He had no protection against being deprived of his appointment. During the war many thousands of officers had been so dealt with. All officers were amenable to that procedure. It was well understood and hardly ever challenged. It was not challenged by General Dyer.'

The second method, pointed out the Secretary of State for War, was of a more serious character, because it affected, not the officer's employment, but his status and rank. It was a question of retiring an officer compulsorily or imposing some forfeiture in pay or pension.

The third method was one of definitely penal character because honour, liberty and life were affected. Cashiering, imprisonment or even the death penalty might be involved.

In respect to the case of General Dyer, Mr Churchill pointed out:

'He was removed from his appointment by the Commander-in-Chief in India; he was passed over by the Selection Board for promotion; he was informed there were no prospects of further employment, and in consequence he reverted automatically to half-pay. The India Office and the Commander-in-Chief recommended that he should be ordered to retire. These recommendations were brought to the attention of the Army Council. They asked Dyer to make a statement, for it was essential that he should be judged upon it. They had to deal with such matters from a military point of view, to express an opinion from a service standpoint.'

The Army Council, he said, considered that, in spite of the great difficulty of the position with which he had been faced on April 13th, Dyer could not be acquitted of an error of judgment. They accepted the decision of the Commander-in-Chief, India, that he should revert to half-pay and they did not consider that further employment should be offered to him outside India. It was an unanimous decision, Mr Churchill told the House, and one that spoke for itself. The Cabinet accepted that decision.

Dealing with the situation in April 1919, Mr Churchill rejected the idea that Dyer saved India. There were more British troops in the country than at the time of the Mutiny, and they were supported by appliances which did not then exist, airplanes, railways and wireless, which gave increased means of concentrating troops with almost undreamed of facilities. He could not conceal from the House, he said, his sincere personal opinion that General Dyer's conduct deserved not only the loss of employment from which so many officers were then suffering, not only the measure of censure which the Government had pronounced, but 'also that it should have been marked by a distinct disciplinary act, namely his being placed compulsorily upon the retired list'. But, pointed out Mr Churchill, in face of the condonation given to his conduct by his superiors, it could not have been possible or right to take disciplinary action against him.

Dyer, who was accompanied by Sir Michael O'Dwyer, listened to the debate. The strength of the vote in his favour was cheering, but the Government had won the first round. One glimmer of hope remained; his case would be debated also in the calmer atmosphere of the House of Lords, by men, many of them soldiers and ex-colonial administrators, who might the better understand the situation with which he was faced; by men less susceptible to the clamour of the Indian politicians, the fermentors of the rebellion he had crushed, the wolves, to conciliate whom, he believed, the Government had thrown him.

Dyer had saved India. The Government had treated him disgracefully, vindictively, clamoured the *Morning Post* on the day following the debate in the Commons. In an 'Appeal to Patriots' it announced the inauguration of a subscription to enable the British public to show their sympathy for Dyer and their disgust for the way he had been treated by an ungrateful Government. Dyer was adverse at first to the appeal and he asked the opinion of Sir Michael O'Dwyer, who reassured him, and O'Dwyer and Sir Edward Carson, who had led his supporters in the Commons, started the fund with a contribution of £20 each. Within twelve hours £584 8s 4d had been raised and in the next four weeks an avalanche of money poured in, in sums great, small and even tiny, accompanied by shoals of letters from every type of person, all acclaiming Dyer as the gallant soldier who had saved India, an overwhelming vote of popular confidence, a singular act of faith, unexampled in modern times.

A 'governess' sent 1s, a 'patriot' £25, a 'sympathiser' £2 2s, an anonymous donor 10d, a 'poor gentleman 2s 6d, one of the 'new poor' 2s 6d, 'fifty years in India' £25, an 'old soldier' £10, a 'country parson' 3s, a 'mutiny widow' 5s, a 'widow and her daughter who know more about Amritsar than Mr Montagu' 12s 6d, 'anti-Jew' (a dig at the Secretary of State for India) 10s 6d, 'a beggar who loves justice' 1s, 'two very poor old ladies' 1s. There were hundreds of gifts of 2s 6d, 1s 6d and 1s, and many larger ones; the Duke of Bedford gave £100, the Duke of Northumberland £25, Horatio Bottomley £50; 1s came from 'three indignant but hard-up schoolgirls', 1s from 'the granddaughter and great-grand-daughter of Indian Army officers', 1s from an officer in Peshawar 'who knew what the situation was', £12 12s from an 'indignant sympathiser'. In India £500 was raised for the fund. Day by day the total mounted, £9,000, £13,894, £14,000, £19,057. In a month the prodigious sum of £26,317 had been collected, a fortune in 1920, a golden handshake for the 'Hero of the Hour' from the people of Britain.

Dyer's case came up for debate in the 'freer and more impartial atmosphere of the House of Lords', as Sir Michael O'Dwyer calls it, on July 19th and 20th, and he observes it was significant that many Law Lords who joined in the debate, with one exception, either supported Dyer's action or condemned the procedure by which he had been censured and punished. Dyer and his staunch supporter listened to the discussion of the firing in the Jallianwala Bagh.

Several peers attempted to justify Dyer's action on the ground that the insurrectionary movement was widespread and it was his duty to crush it. It was not a mere local riot in Amritsar.

In respect to the claim that Dyer had been put at a disadvantage by the Indian members of the Committee, Lord Sinha, the Under-Secretary of State for India, pointed out that his most damaging statements had been made to Lord Hunter, a suggestion which brought the observation from another peer that Dyer's frankness had been the cause of his undoing.

The Marquess of Crewe, a former Secretary of State for War, submitted that Dyer's argument that he had been faced with a rival army was hardly tenable. It was hard to understand, he said, how his 1,200 troops, armed with guns, could have been swept away. The risk of his troops being mobbed in the Jallianwala Bagh was not great. He went on to point out: 'If it be that with an inadequate force you can only deal with a crowd by starting to shoot at it, and continuing to shoot at it as long as your ammunition holds out, that seems, of itself, to be a condemnation of your going with that particular force to disperse that crowd at all. It is surely a most dangerous argument to use, that because your force is a small one you may legitimately employ methods which a larger force would not think of employing. To what would that argument lead? Poison-gas would disperse a much larger crowd very quickly with a much smaller number of men, but nobody suggests that it should be adopted as a means of dealing with unlawful gatherings, however forcibly, by proclamation or otherwise, you have announced your intention to punish them.' Dyer, he suggested, had taken a wrong turning.

The only stigma cast upon Dyer, declared the Lord Chancellor, the Earl of Birkenhead, was that he had committed a tragic error of judgment. He had been subjected, he observed, to the mildest disciplinary action known to the Army. He had said himself there was no danger of his force being rushed. He fired on a mass of humanity which had begun to run. He personally directed the fire to where the number trying to escape was thickest. They were trying to disperse, the very thing he said he wanted them to do. That did not exhaust what General Dyer wanted to do, he remarked:

'He has told us his theory in language that is absolutely unmistakable and it has relieved us from any necessity for speculating on the matter. He said, "If I had had more weapons there would have been more casualties". What does that mean? It means that the only limit to the casualties he would have thought it right to inflict were the number of weapons that he could provide, and he makes it quite plain that if he had been able to get his armoured motor cars, which he took with him, inside Jallianwala Bagh, he would have used the machine-guns upon that crowd in precisely the same way that he used the rifles.'

Such a course of conduct cannot be defended, emphasized the Lord Chancellor, and he stated the opinion that it was not for an officer of the rank of Colonel, acting as a Brigadier-General, to take upon himself the responsibility of arriving at decisions and basing action not upon the immediate local necessity but upon the political conditions of the whole of a vast population like the Punjab.

Lord Meston, a member of the Government of India in April 1919, dealt with the argument that there had been great delay in dealing with the case. He would endeavour to picture the condition of the country, he told the House.

'The situation was that as the result of unpopular legislation in March at Delhi a violent, unscrupulous political agitation burst out over the whole length and breadth of India—a type of agitation with which we are unfortunately familiar. There was a sudden and dramatic transition to organized violence. That violence focused in the Central and Northern Punjab and one of its most characteristic features was the determination showed by the insurgents to destroy communications.'

For a time, he said, the Government of India at Simla was isolated and he explained how on the afternoon of the 13th they received an appeal from O'Dwyer for permission to initiate martial law, which came by wireless, because every single wire to Simla was cut. He told the House, 'I remember the anxiety we felt that afternoon as to whether we should be able to get the reply back to him in time, because a local thunderstorm had upset the working of the little wireless installation near Simla'.

Officers were few, he explained, staffs depleted by the war and by the rush of leave following it. Then came the Afghan invasion. General Dyer was transferred to the frontier, while the Government of India was still unaware of the unfortunate aspects of what he had done at Amritsar. It was not until August, when he sent in his report, that the Government knew what had really happened. He himself, he said, in April had the impression that the 200 casualties mentioned by Dyer meant 50 dead and 150 wounded, in accordance with the ordinary ratio. An enquiry could not be undertaken at once. A distinguished judicial officer from England was required. The Viceroy, he said, made up his mind to hold an enquiry within a fortnight of the Amritsar affair. A decision about Dyer was postponed until that enquiry reported. Had there been any active condonation of Dyer's action? Lord Meston asked. The message of the Lieutenant-Governor, he said, was sent in complete ignorance of the whole circumstance. At the meeting of the Legislative Council in September the officials who spoke were not concerned with defending individual acts but with the justification of martial law for the purpose of urging the passing of the Indemnity Act. There was, he said, no defined or assumed approval of those acts which the Government of India now condemned. There was anything but deliberate condonation of an act subsequently disavowed, he said. The Government of India had not spoken with two voices to General Dyer.

Turning to the graver charges, that Dyer had been treated with injustice and his treatment would deter other officers from doing their duty, Lord Meston said he wished to concede every point it was possible to concede in General Dyer's favour. When he came to Amritsar, a heavy, too heavy, and improper responsibility was thrown on him by the abdication of the civil power. He marched to the Jallianwala Bagh expecting to find a defiant and dangerous mob. Let us concede, said Lord Meston, that there was justification for Dyer opening fire, as a sheer necessity of self-preservation. Once the danger was over and the crowd cowed, let us make the further concession that some punishment was warranted. But to such punishment there was a limit. When the crowd was broken and seeking only to escape, that limit was reached. General Dyer passed that limit, claimed Lord Meston. He went on firing until his cartridge belts were almost empty and the ground was covered with dead and wounded. Could there be any possible justification for that?, he asked, and he put it to the House:

'There was a point, in other words, up to which firing may have been necessary, probably was necessary in the circumstances. There was a further point up to which firing may have been justifiable as a stern, sharp punishment for persistent lawlessness, but beyond that point further firing was vengeance, and it was as vengeance that General Dyer subsequently described and defended it. Here, therefore, I submit that our justification must stop.'

It was said that Dyer had saved a mutiny. That was clearly a wrong word, Lord Meston suggested, because the Indian Army remained staunch. Dyer relied upon Indian troops to execute his punishments, and they obeyed their orders unflinchingly. Nor did he avert a general conflagration, for the great majority of the population remained loyal. The insurgents were defeated, he asserted, not by Dyer's bullets but by the steadfast front shown by the Government. General Dyer's action, commented Lord Meston, had recoiled upon us in bitterness, in sadness and in disgust in India.

In the House of Lords, Dyer was supported by eight dukes, six marquesses, thirty-one earls, ten viscounts, and seventy-four barons. Against the motion voted the Archbishop of Canterbury, the Lord Chancellor, two marquesses, nineteen earls, fifteen viscounts and forty-six barons.

The House of Lords had voted for him by a large majority. Dyer must have been elated. Here was vindication, justification for his action, support tremendous and powerful. A hundred and twenty-nine Lords, and a similar number of Members of the House of Commons, 258 of the most influential men in Britain, stood by him. Thousands of ordinary men and women were demonstrating their support, too, by their contributions to the *Morning Post* Fund. He had been right, the Government had treated him unjustly. He had saved India; he was the 'Hero of the Hour'. The terrible conflicting doubts his treatment had created dissolved. The dark shadow of the Jallianwala Bagh faded from Dyer's mind.

XVI

LIBEL

The House of Lords' vote, the tenor of the speeches made, and the support of General Dyer by a large section of the British public 'shocked' Indian opinion, says Sir George Barrow, and Bishop Whitehead of Madras (*Indian Problems*) found that his Indian friends 'felt so bitterly on the subject that they would not trust themselves to speak about it in the presence of Europeans'. Indians of all classes, says Sir Valentine Chirol (*India*), would not believe that, if such actions had been taken against a mob in an English town, 'the British public would not have been as unanimous in reprobating them as Indian opinion was in this case'. Mr Edward Thompson, the correspondent of the *Manchester Guardian*, reported that the exoneration of Dyer in the Lords 'aroused unspeakable indignation in India and rendered the task of the Indian Government almost impossible' (*The Reconstruction of India*). Rabindranath Tagore (*Letters to a Friend*) wrote from London on July 22nd:

'The result of the Dyer debates in both Houses of Parliament makes painfully evident the attitude of mind of the ruling classes of the country towards India. It shows that no outrage, however monstrous, committed against us by the agents of their Government, can arouse feelings of indignation in the hearts of those from whom our governors are chosen. The unashamed condonation of brutality expressed in their speeches and echoed in their newspapers is ugly in its frightfulness. The late events have conclusively proved that our true salvation lies in our own hands; that a nation's greatness can never find its foundation in half-hearted concessions of contemptuous niggardliness.'

When in February 1921 the Duke of Connaught, representing the King, opened the Parliament of India, he found it necessary to say 'The shadow of Amritsar has lengthened over the fair face of India', and the first act of the new Parliament was to move a resolution dealing with the Punjab episode, in which, says Edward Thompson, the Government spokesman had to speak with unusual emphasis to make clear 'the deep regret of the administration at the perpetration of those improper actions, and their firm determination that, as far as human foresight could avail, any repetition would be forever impossible'. The Home Minister, Sir William Vincent, he says 'repudiated emphatically the suggestion that Indian lives were valued more lightly than the lives of Englishmen', and he expressed his deep regret 'that the canons of conduct for which the British administration stood had been violated by some of the acts of certain individual officers'.

Writing from India to the *Daily Telegraph* on March 1, 1921, on the 'Amritsar Incident', Percival Landon told his readers 'there is scarcely a hut where the story has not been told'. Dyer's action, he stated, had unconsciously changed the whole course of events for 'then it was, in despair of achieving anything against us in the open field, that Gandhi, with his policy of non-violence, ascended to the throne of sedition'. That was the most important result of the Amritsar trouble, Landon declared. Violence had been tried and found useless; non-co-operation was a far more effective way to drive out the English. 'It is not to be forgotten that when at Amritsar Dyer crushed a rebellion, he paved the way for the undisputed supremacy of Gandhi', Landon emphasized.

Stating his opinion in 1937, Reginald Reynolds (*The White Sahibs in India*) says that the blood of Amritsar was the seed of the national Congress which, from a policy of co-operation, swung to non-co-operation, and Gandhi became the 'voice of the Indian people'. Michael Edwards, in *A History of India*, says that Amritsar turned Gandhi into a revolutionary, but one never seen before, and that he gave the nationalistic movement a revolutionary impetus by his policy of non-co-operation.

At Amritsar, the Jallianwala Bagh was purchased from its thirty-four individual owners for Rs.500,000, raised by national subscription, and consecrated as an Indian National Memorial.

Returning to England we learn from Mr Colvin that, after the House of Lords debate, Dyer fell into a state of despondency from which it was difficult to arouse him. He went to Harrogate for treatment and then to the farm in Gloucestershire which he had bought for his son, Geoffrey. 'He was suffering from arterial sclerosis, something too deep to cure', relates his biographer.

On December 6, 1920, a cheque for £26,317 arrived from the *Morning Post*, accompanied by a letter from the Editor, who told Dyer that the sum would be a welcome proof 'that your conduct has met with the approval of a large number of your countrymen', although, he remarked, 'no sum of money can possibly repay the debt the Empire owes you'. To this message Dyer replied, 'I am proud to think that so many of my fellow countrymen and women approve of my conduct', and he told the Morning Post's readers, 'on my part my conviction was, and still is, that I was bound to do what I did, not only with a view to saving the military situation and the women and children, but with a view to saving life generally. No hesitation or half-hearted measures would, under the circumstances, have served the purpose. The act I was called upon to perform filled me with horror, but the great sympathy and approval accorded me by thousands strengthen my convictions and they are a great help to me at a time of extreme pain.'

In a leading article headed 'A Debt Acknowledged', the Morning Post stated that by the contributions which had come from every part of the globe 'the stigma of national ingratitude has been in part removed', and the newspaper recorded its opinion that General Dyer had 'faced the ordeal without flinching'. He was not weak, but humane.

In rural Gloucestershire, Dyer worked upon his book The Raiders of the Sarhad, and he contributed an article to The Globe, which published it on January 21, 1921; India's Path to Suicide, in which he declared the attempt to overthrow the British Raj was 'well-planned'. Self-government for India was, he said, a 'horrible pretence', for under it 'She would commit suicide and our politicians would be guilty of murder as associates in the crime'. India did not want and did not understand self-government, he stated, and he gave his opinion that to the massed millions of India, 'the Raj is immaculate, just and strong, to them the British officer is a Sahib, who will do them right and protect them from enemies of all kinds. Of course, if the Raj suffers itself to be wantonly flouted and insulted, it is no longer the Raj at all. And it is when that happens that the extremists get their chance.' Those in high places who paid attention to the demands of Indian extremists, he said, were either vote catching or frightened of long shadows. An Eleventh Commandment should be applied to India, he suggested, 'Thou shalt not agitate'. The agitators, he declared, were not the ruling classes of India and they were incapable of checking or controlling the storm they sought to excite. If it came to bloodshed, the first to flow would be that of Gandhi and his friends. The Indians, he stated, would not be capable of self-government for generations, and if they made India unbearable for the British then 'Indians will wade through a sea of blood'. Dyer appealed to his fellow citizens to let a just and strong will be established in India 'to prevent political considerations at home from weakening the hands of our rulers, great and small, in India'. Gandhi, he said, would not lead India to capable self-government. 'A new star has not risen in the East, a new era will not come suddenly', he claimed, and British rule must continue firm and unshaken. In a brief reference to the disorders of 1919 he said the rebellion was well timed and well planned, adding it was fortunate that 'We in the Punjab had time to act'. These are opinions which may help us to understand Dyer's character.

In November 1921, says his biographer, Dyer was struck down by paralysis, followed by thrombosis, and he suffered from weakness and depression. The disease from which Dyer suffered, we recall, is stated by Mr Colvin to have been 'arterial sclerosis' and that diagnosis may be a guide to our understanding of his action at the Jallianwala Bagh, and the conflicting reasons he gave for it.

It was held by Mr Justice Devlin (now Lord Devlin) in the case of R. v. Kemp [(1957) 1. Queens Bench 399] that the accused, who was charged with causing grievous bodily harm to his wife, and who suffered from arteriosclerosis (hardening of the arteries), leading to a congestion of blood on the brain and causing a temporary loss of consciousness, came within the test of the McNaghton Rules and was insane. Kemp, who displayed no sign of mental trouble, attacked his wife when temporarily unconscious from a congestion of blood on the brain. The judge intimated that a disease capable of affecting the mind in such a way as to cause a defect, temporarily or permanently, of its reasoning, understanding and so on, was a disease of the mind within the Rules.

We may legitimately speculate whether Dyer's mental condition existed sufficiently in April 1919 to impair his judgment, and reduce his responsibility for the action he took, and the explanations he gave for it, which are so difficult to understand.

Dyer was too ill in 1924 to give evidence, or even to be told of the course of the trial, in the action for libel brought by Sir Michael O'Dwyer against Sir C. Sankaran Nair, whose book *Gandhi and Anarchy*, published in 1922, libelled him. Fortunately, says O'Dwyer, the opportunity presented itself to obtain the verdict of a British judge and jury on the whole question of the Punjab 'atrocities', including Dyer's action at Amritsar. Sir Sankaran Nair, O'Dwyer explains, was formerly a judge of the Madras High Court, and a Member of the Government of India from 1915 to July 1919, when he agreed to the imposition of martial law.

On his resignation, which increased his popularity with the advanced Indian politicians with whom he had been closely associated, says O'Dwyer, Nair came to England and was selected by Mr Montagu as one of his colleagues in the India Council. In the Moplah rebellion, which occurred in Malabar in 1920, O'Dwyer observes, Nair advocated far more drastic measures of repression than he had done in the Punjab. Seeing the dangers of Gandhi's movement, Nair resigned his position on the India Council and took up the post of adviser to the state of Indore. There he wrote his book, in which, according to O'Dwyer, he vigorously denounced the non-co-operation movement as fatal to the political progress of India. 'All this was to the good, though rather belated', says O'Dwyer, who adds: 'If the book had stopped there, it would have had my hearty approval as I had been preaching the same doctrine for three years previously. But for some reason Sir Sankaran Nair thought it advisable to go out of his way to attack me in the following passages.'

In the action he brought against Nair, O'Dwyer cited three passages which, he declared, were defamatory to him. These accused him of 'terrorism' in recruitment during the war, of committing 'atrocities' in the Punjab during the suppression of the disorders, of 'high handed' proceedings, and Nair stated that the 'eulogium passed by the English Cabinet on Lord Chelmsford and Sir Michael O'Dwyer was an outrage on Indian public opinion'. Innuendoes which, when made by a former member of the Government of India, O'Dwyer could not pass by.

After lengthy preliminary proceedings, in which sworn statements were taken from witnesses in India, and O'Dwyer was refused, he says, the use of documents by the India Office on the ground that their publication would be prejudicial to the public interest, or allowed the use only of censored copies, the action came for trial in London in May and June, 1924, before Mr Justice McCardie and a special jury.

In the Royal Courts of Justice there were once again gathered the men who had been prominent in the suppression of the Punjab disorders, with the exception of General Dyer, the one who above all was once again on trial, now at last, as his friends had so long desired, before an impartial British judge and jury. With the chief issue of the action, Sir Michael O'Dwyer's actions, we are not concerned: he won his case and he was vindicated completely. 'The action of General Dyer at Amritsar and my responsibility in the matter was one of the chief issues of the trial', says O'Dwyer. His counsel at its start stated that it was impossible to call Dyer as a witness because he was ill and not expected to live.

The question whether Dyer acted rightly or wrongly was for them to decide, Mr Justice McCardie told the jury. He would express his own opinion, he stated. And in words, 'delivered with a solemnity which thrilled the hushed Court', records Sir Michael O'Dwyer, 'the judge spoke with the voice of justice'.

'Speaking with full deliberation and knowing the whole of the evidence given in this case, I express my view that General Dyer, in the grave and exceptional circumstances, acted rightly, and in my opinion he was wrongly punished by the Secretary of State for India. That is my view and I need scarcely say that I have weighed every circumstance and every detail which was not before the Hunter Committee.'

'As His Lordship concluded', says Sir Michael O'Dwyer, 'the tension in the hushed audience gave way to an involuntary murmur of subdued applause. It was felt that after five years of suppression or misrepresentation of the facts the truth had at last been established. British justice had triumphed, a cruel wrong had been righted. But vindication came too late. General Dyer is shattered in health, a broken man.'

The jury, by a majority verdict of eleven to one, voted in favour of Sir Michael O'Dwyer, and by implication for General Dyer. Mrs Dyer, records Mr Colvin, was allowed by the doctor to tell her husband the result of the case, and he says, 'It greatly consoled him, but an incurable illness took its inevitable course'.

The jury's verdict and the judge's emphatic opinion were taken by many people to settle the controversy about General Dyer, states Sir George Barrow. But it was only one man's opinion, he stresses. No more. The jury, he points out, were not asked to decide whether Dyer had committed an atrocity, but whether O'Dwyer had, which was really a different question. The judge, unlike the Hunter Committee, he observes, had not heard and seen all the witnesses or visited the places where the actions happened. Sir George Barrow might have drawn the attention of his readers to another point. The claim that the libel action disclosed fresh evidence about Dyer's action is a myth; no new facts were brought to light.

The impact of the verdict in India, and the judge's statement (which the *Tribune* called 'a wanton misuse of judicial authority'), further lacerated the feelings already torn by the House of Lords debate, and its outcome, and Mr Justice McCardie's statement of judicial opinion, placed the British Government in an awkward position, one which was made even more difficult by the question put in the House of Commons by Colonel Sir Charles Yate, who prayed 'that this judicial opinion and finding, based upon a full consideration of all the evidence, be accepted, and that His Majesty will be graciously pleased to revoke the censure passed upon General Dyer after the incomplete executive investigation in 1920'. 'No, Sir', replied the Prime Minister, Mr Ramsay MacDonald, 'I am not prepared to grant time for the discussion of this motion.'

The Secretary of State for India, Lord Oliver, found it advisable to send a special dispatch to the Government of India, disavowing the judge's opinion in respect to General Dyer's action.

General Dyer's action had been supported at first by his superiors, and both General Sir William Beynon and Sir Michael O'Dwyer stuck to the opinions they had originally voiced. He had been censured by the Hunter Committee, whose disapproval of his conduct was confirmed by the Government of India and by the British Government. He had been retired from the Army. On the other hand 129 Members of the Commons and 129 Lords supported him, as had thousands of his fellow countrymen. Now, a judge and jury had vindicated him.

We can now turn to the question: Which was Dyer, the Hero of the Hour, the soldier who saved India, or the Villain of the Piece, the man who had wantonly shot down some 1,500 defenceless and unresisting Indians?

XVII

THE STORY ENDS WITH MURDER

General Dyer died on July 23, 1927. His body was brought to London and accorded a military funeral at the Church of St Martins-in-the-Fields. His principal supporter, Sir Michael O'Dwyer, survived him by thirteen years. Then on March 13, 1940, he fell victim to an assassin's bullet. O'Dwyer was shot dead by an Indian named Udham Singh, who said his real name was Singh Azad, at the Caxton Hall, London, at the end of a meeting called by the East India Association and the Royal Central Asian Society. Udham Singh, who with other shots wounded Lord Zetland, the Secretary of State for India, a former Governor of Bombay, Lord Lamington, and Sir Louis Dane, a former Lieutenant-Governor of the Punjab, was seized and overpowered.

At his trial for murder on June 5th and 6th, he pleaded that the shooting was accidental; someone jerked his arm as he was about to fire at the ceiling as a protest against the treatment of Indians by the British. He said he was aged sixteen in 1919, living in the Punjab, and he remembered the shooting incident at Amritsar; it was one of the things which made him hate British rule. But he declared he did not know that the man he killed was then the Lieutenant-Governor of the Punjab, a statement belied by his possession of O'Dwyer's address at Thurlestone, Devon. Several disjointed statements made by Udham Singh to the police, who may have understood them imperfectly, due to his poor command of English, seemed to increase further the belief that he intended to kill O'Dwyer. He was alleged to have said, 'I did it because I had a grudge against him. He deserved it. I am dying for my country.' He was convicted and hanged, his counsel pointing out that probably in no other country in the world and at that critical time (the height of the evacuation of the British Army from Dunkirk) would a vehement opponent of imperialism be afforded so calm and fair a trial by a court of the empire he denounced.

Whether or not Udham Singh's revolver shots were a final echo of the firing in the Jallianwala Bagh, we can now turn to consider the problems which the evidence has disclosed, whether Dyer's action was right or wrong, what were his true motives, whether his condemnation was justified, and the extraordinary support he received from a large and influential section of the British public.

One piece of evidence still remains to be considered. In his book, *A Letter from India*, Mr Edward Thompson, an acknowledged authority on India, tells us:

'Jalianwalabagh has profoundly affected all who have seen it. A dozen years ago, a distinguished soldier and explorer, who justified General Dyer's action to me—"It was Prussianism; but, then, Prussianism is necessary"—added that another soldier who had been even more pro-Dyer than himself had returned from Amritsar saying, "I'll never say another word. It was sheer massacre."'

'The outside world has never had the slightest conception of the intensity of feeling in April 1919', says Mr Thompson, and he continues:

'Over a dozen years I have met an exceptional number of men who were close to what happened and have known intimately protagonists of both sides. Much of what I have been told I cannot pass on. But some facts hidden hitherto ought to be known. Indian minds have been outraged by the memory of General Dyer's brutal, purposeful massacre, as revealed in his own testimony. They have been carrying a burden greater than the truth warranted . . .

'Mr Miles Irving, now Commissioner of Lahore, was Deputy Commissioner of Amritsar in 1919. General Dyer did not let him know of his purpose before going to Jalianwalabagh. A chance sentence that I heard in Delhi made me anxious to know more of what happened afterwards. Dining with Mr Irving, when five of us—Mr Irving, Mr F. G. Puckle (Financial Secretary, Punjab Government), Sir Abdul Qadir, Mr Schuyler (an American educational missionary) and myself—were together after dinner, I said to Mr Irving, "I have been wanting to ask you a very improper question. What did General Dyer say to you after Jalianwalabagh?" He replied, "Dyer came to me all dazed and shaken up, and said, 'I never knew that there was no way out'." He explained that when the crowd did not scatter but held its ground he thought it was massing to attack him, so kept on firing. Mr Puckle now said that six months later General Dyer came through his station and dined with him, and told him, "I haven't had a night's sleep since that happened. I keep on seeing it all over again."

'I have never doubted that General Dyer's action saved the Punjab from a revolt, with its attendant horrors. Nor have I ever doubted that it did irreparable mischief to the Raj, and that he shot away more than he preserved. His deed was appalling—firing into that crowd as we can visualize them, without realizing that there must be something wrong when they did not race away. Yet we may dismiss once for all the belief that he was anti-Indian or a man naturally cruel. The man who "kept on seeing" what had happened was neither of these things. In justice both to him and to human nature we should remember that he went to Jalianwala straight from news of murder and arson and resolved to act sternly, but that he never planned the slaughter that ensued. He "never knew that there was no way out".

'Seven months elapsed before the Hunter Inquiry. He found that in the tragic intensity of men's emotions he was regarded as a hero. The disorders had ceased instantaneously, and an alternative presented itself to his first dreadful thought that he had blundered. Pressure of outside congratulation helped him to build up the conviction that he saved the Empire. The witnesses before the Hunter Commission stood lonely before their examiners, in a court filled with angry hearers. "There is no doubt that Dyer was trailing his coat" (said Mr Irving), which, indeed, is very obvious. He refused to listen to advice, and took his own line of insistence on playing a martyr's role.

'The story of the last dozen years would have been immeasurably happier had we realized that Jalianwalabagh was the scene of a mistake and not of calculated brutality. I asked Mr Irving, "Why was not the Hunter Commission told what he had said?" He made the perfectly natural answer, "Do you know, Dyer and I both clean forgot. I was being questioned hard about other things" (and it must be remembered a witness's job is to answer questions put to him and not to divagate' "and he was determined to fight." I asked further, "Have you any objection to my publishing what you have told me?" "None", he replied.

'General Dyer made his own legend of what he had done, and he imposed it on the world; and no man ever made a worse mess of his own case. The Lytton Strachey of 1952 will find an absorbing psychological study ready to his hand. Dyer persuaded himself and us that he went to Jalianwala determined on deliberate massacre. It simply is not true. He went to do the job of an officer called in to suppress disorder with which the civil authorities could not cope. The rest happened as I have said.'

Mr Nehru, on the other hand, who visited the Jallianwala Bagh on numerous occasions shortly after the shooting, denies this explanation of Dyer's conduct:

'A suggestion has been made, I think by Mr Edward Thompson, that General Dyer was under the impression that there were other exits from the Bagh and it was because of this that he continued his firing for so long. Even if that was Dyer's impression, and there were in fact some exits, that would hardly lessen his responsibility. But it seems very strange that he should have such an impression. Any person, standing on the raised ground where he stood, could have a good view of the entire space and could see how shut in it was on all sides by houses several storeys high. Only on one side, for a hundred feet or so, there was no house, but a low wall about five feet high. With a murderous fire mowing them down and unable to find a way out, thousands of people rushed to this wall and tried to climb over it. The fire was then directed, it appears (both from our evidence and innumerable bullet marks on the wall itself), towards this wall to prevent people escaping over it. And when all was over, some of the biggest heaps of dead and wounded lay on either side of this wall.'

In attempting to assess Dyer's action in the Jallianwala Bagh, and his motives for firing, two salient facts stand out; he fired to disperse the crowd without warning and, after it had started to disperse, he went on firing until his ammunition was nearly exhausted. He ceased fire, apparently, not because he had killed enough, but because his ammunition was getting low.

It may be conceded that an order to disperse might have been ignored, or not heard, and that some firing may have been necessary to disperse the crowd, some of whom had gathered in defiance of the proclamation. Dyer, we may argue, should have broadcast his proclamation more widely, and he should not have assumed that everyone in the illegal assembly knew of it. Whether the crowd was advised of his approach, thus constituting a warning, as Dyer surmised, is unknown. But, it may be asked, if it was warned, and if it was a rebellious gathering, a potential 'bludgeon army', as Dyer claimed, why did it not take steps to bar his entry? The assembly clearly comprised some, at least, of the rioters who had committed murder and arson two days previously, and it may be assumed that it was not an entirely innocent gathering, for the purpose of airing grievances. But it is necessary to recall that no excesses had been committed for two days, and no attempt had been made to attack the troops on their various excursions into the city. It is possible that the riots were dying out as suddenly as they had arisen, and that, had Dyer left well alone, Amritsar might have returned to normal within a few days.

But a soldier in his position could hardly adopt such a negative attitude, especially as he had good reason to believe that the disorders were spreading elsewhere, and that attempts were being made to isolate him and his small force. It was advisable, also, to regain control of the city by some positive act and the illegal meeting provided a golden opportunity to show the people, by its dispersal, that the authorities were once again in control. But that was no excuse for punishing the crowd, far less for setting out to create a widespread moral effect.

Dyer thought that the disorders which broke out simultaneously throughout the Punjab, and in other parts of India, were part of a concerted, centrally organized, movement, which it was his duty to suppress by a strong act. He admitted he had no evidence of such a conspiracy, and the Hunter Committee, who heard the evidence, failed to detect it. Whether they considered all the testimony is open to question, but none the less, it seems clear that the disorders, which in places developed into open defiance of authority, thereby constituting legal 'rebellion', were local and spontaneous, sudden manifestations of the eruption of dissatisfaction which followed the war. In Amritsar they were certainly spontaneous and local, and they were brought on by the deportation of the people's leaders which led to an outburst of indignation which resulted inevitably in members of the mob being killed, which so incensed their companions that violent excesses were committed in the heat of the moment. The situation was grave, but its dangers were probably over-estimated. Ill-advisedly, the civil authorities abdicated control in favour of inexperienced soldiers.

When he learned of the illegal meeting, it was Dyer's duty to break it up. At the same time, it provided him with the opportunity which, according to his biographer, he had been seeking; to bring the mob out into the open and to do something strong. But, whatever were his motives, he far exceeded his duty; to shoot down 1,500 unresisting people, killing 379 of them, was, as Mr Churchill aptly called it, a 'monstrous event'. The only justification for such an action was the fear that his force was in danger and might be wiped out, with all the terrible consequences that eventuality implied. If he had no such fear, or any reason for it, Dyer's action was wrong, and nothing that was said then or can be said now can absolve him from blame, the charge that he continued firing after the frightened people had taken to flight, particularly as he himself said he could have dispersed the assembly without firing. No doubt his action was successful; it ended the disorders everywhere, but it neither saved the Punjab nor all India from conflagration, and in fact it did grave disservice to British rule, and it contributed in no small part to its termination twenty-eight years later.

Dyer apparently committed an atrocity, which the Hunter Committee forbearingly called an 'error of judgment'. But can an atrocity be committed by a man who acted with complete integrity and honesty of purpose? It seems probable that Dyer was, in Sir George Barrow's words, an 'honest soldier', a man 'whose fault lay in a failure to show, in a difficult situation, the judgment which is required in the army of an officer of his rank'. Sir George Barrow expressed his belief that Dyer acted in 'good faith'. Dyer was certainly no drooling monster, or bloodthirsty tyrant, seeking mere revenge, committing intentionally an atrocity for which no excuse is possible. It is only by his intentions that Dyer can be judged, but he has left us in considerable doubt as to what were his true reasons for continuing to fire on the fleeing crowd.

According to Mr Miles Irving, who died in June 1962, if we accept Mr Thompson's statement, Dyer's first and earliest reaction to the firing was to say that the crowd was trying to rush him, a misapprehension he gained from what we now know was his mistaken belief that there were adequate exits from the Bagh. He thought, apparently, in this interpretation, that the crowd, baffled of means of escape, was determined to attack him. In other words, in continuing to fire, Dyer made an error, an understandable one if he believed there were other exits from the Bagh, a supposed belief on his part which is strengthened by the tradition held in the army that Dyer had been told there were 'two gates' in the Jallianwala Bagh, the one he entered by and another, or others, at the far end, one of which, he was not told, had been blocked up. On the other hand this tradition may be no more than a service 'myth', created in exculpation of the officer for whose conduct the army found it necessary to find an excuse. Whether or not Dyer, incorrectly as it happened, was led to believe that there were other exits, we cannot tell now, but we may recall that he was accompanied to the Bagh by the Superintendent of Police and the Assistant Commissioner, both of whom presumably knew the place well. According to Mr. Nehru, Dyer could hardly have suffered from such a misapprehension.

Dyer's apparent early belief that the crowd came surging back to rush him is confirmed by the statements he made a few days later. To Sir Michael O'Dwyer he said he thought the crowd was trying to get behind him, and to General Beynon he explained he thought they were gathering for a rush, two slightly different explanations which suggest that Dyer's memory was confused. He made no mention to either of his misconception of the geography of the Bagh, and his reported remark to the Deputy Commissioner is the last we hear of the most plausible of his early explanations. His exlanation that he believed his force stood in actual danger has the benefit of being the earliest one, which in such cases is often the true story, and it is confirmed by Captain Briggs who stated in his report: 'We began to fire upon the crowd, which broke into two bodies. Things were getting very serious indeed, and it looked as though they were gathering for a rush. Fire was ordered first on one lump of crowd which looked the most menacing and then on the other.'

It is curious to find, therefore, that when he came to write his own report on April 14th, within twenty-four hours of the event, Dyer had no better explanation to offer than to say that, as his force was small, 'to hesitate might induce attack'. He did not suggest that he had been in fear of attack, or that any hostile movement had been made by the crowd. He made no attempt to justify his action, a strange omission considering that a few days later he had explanations to offer. In the proclamation, issued in the name of the Deputy Commissioner, to dispel the rumours about the incident, it was said only that 'the people showed an attitude of defiance'.

Four months then elapsed, during which time Dyer was acclaimed as the Saviour of India, and, according to Sir George Barrow, he talked a lot about his action and 'over-brooded' upon it, and on August 25th he came up with an entirely different explanation. He made no suggestion of there being any emergency or anything in the demeanour of the crowd which compelled him to fire, and he denied his earlier explanation by saying that the crowd was so dense that *if a determined rush had been made*, arms or no arms, his small force must instantly have been overpowered, and consequently he was very careful of *not giving* the mob a chance of organizing. His mind, he said, had been made up, if he found a crowd assembled, to open fire, and it was not a question of merely dispersing the crowd but of punishing it and of producing a moral effect throughout the Punjab. He intended to kill, in order to teach a lesson and create a widespread impression. The act was not forced upon him; he did it deliberately and intentionally. There was no question of undue severity; it was his bounden duty to disperse the unlawful assembly.

Two months later, his explanation to the Hunter Committee was even more arrogant, and he made no attempt to put a favourable complexion upon his action or his purpose. There was no reason to further parley with the mob which had gathered in defiance of his orders. He was going to fire until they dispersed; he continued firing, although they had started to disperse and they might have been dispersed without being fired upon. More casualties might have resulted if he had had more troops or he had been able to bring in his machine guns. If he had not fired the crowd would have laughed at him, made him feel a fool. He said he thought the Bagh had three or four exits, including one wide one, presumably the one by which he had entered, and he made no suggestion that his force had been in danger or that he was apprehensive of being attacked. The crowd had taken no action before he started to fire. His duty had been a horrible, though merciful, one. He had fired to punish the crowd and to strike terror throughout the Punjab. The situation was serious and the province was in rebellion. An explanation which Sir Michael O'Dwyer found 'indefensible', and which neither he nor General Beynon believed to be correct.

When he came to write his statement for the consideration of the Army Council, Dyer had other explanations to offer in justification, the situation on the Afghan frontier, the impending murder of British women and children in the Punjab, the organizing of villagers, the ineffectiveness of the firing on the 10th, the danger to his own force and that the rebellion was a centrally organized movement, one that it was necessary to nip in the bud in Amritsar, the storm centre of revolt. He was faced by a defiant mob, the same mob as had committed the murders on the 10th. It appeared to be collecting into two groups, intending to rush his small force, a revival of his earliest explanation.

Nor must we forget the explanation put forward by Dyer's biographer who, whether or not he knew Dyer, which is not stated, appears to have gathered information from the family. Mr Colvin implies that, prior to the firing in the Jallianwala Bagh, Dyer was anxious to bring the rebels out into the open, and he saw the proposed meeting as an opportunity to end the rebellion by inflicting a crushing blow.

Which of Dyer's explanations is the true one? And why did he change the reasons he gave for continuing to fire?

It is natural that we should wish to find some reasonable explanation for Dyer's conduct which it seems impossible to justify. He was a British officer, a Colonel, an acting Brigadier, who, on his own showing, callously and in cold blood shot down an unarmed and unresisting crowd of natives, directing his fire to where the crowd was thickest, picking off those trying to escape. He gave no warning of his intentions, and he admitted that the crowd might have been dispersed without firing. If he had had stronger means the casualties might have been greater. He fired and continued firing because he feared the crowd might laugh at him, make him feel a fool, not because his troops were in danger. Having nearly exhausted his ammunition, he marched away leaving the wounded to take care of themselves. If the act had been done by a German, a Russian or an Afrikander, we would not bother to seek an explanation. We would probably condemn a man of another race out of hand. Therein lies the danger that we may try too hard to find an excuse for Dyer; because our national pride demands it, we may delude ourselves, we need to realize.

Was Dyer's act a ghastly mistake, or an appalling error of judgment, or was it sheer bloody massacre, an atrocity in the full meaning of the word, a crime against humanity, which we should condemn without question? Did he glory in his deed, as some of his explanations suggest, or did he believe that his small force was in danger?

Dyer believed for the rest of his life he had been right to go on firing. He had to believe that because for his own peace of mind the alternative was too horrible to contemplate. He could not live with the thought, if he ever entertained it, that he might have been wrong. He had to delude himself, and his delusion that he was the Saviour of India was encouraged, and may even have been created, by the praise of his friends. He dropped his original explanation and adopted what seemed to be a better one. If he believed that there were other exits through which the crowd could have escaped and that they turned back to attack him, he committed no worse than a ghastly mistake. If he had stuck to that explanation, all would have been well.

That Dyer could have made such a mistake, and committed such a terrible error, is supported by evidence which suggests that he was a man of poor judgment, which may have been impaired by the onset of the disease which struck him down finally. Arterial sclerosis has a retrograde effect, and it may have been creeping up on him in 1919. If that was so, his judgment, at times of extreme mental stress, may have been so impaired as to diminish his responsibility. He seems to have been prone to outbursts of indignation, such as when he imposed his crawling order and when he had the boys who were suspected only of the assault on Miss Sherwood flogged. Those acts alone suggest that Dyer was victim of some mental disorder, for they are otherwise beyond belief.

Prior to the incident in the Jallianwala Bagh, Dyer had been under extreme tension for two exhausting days. His mind had been inflamed by stories of brutal murder and dastardly assault. He believed the situation to be critical. In Amritsar he was responsible. He and he alone could save the situation in the Punjab. His orders, he learned, had been disobeyed, flouted. He marched to the Jallianwala Bagh, determined to break up the meeting and teach the unruly mob a lesson. To punish them for their disobedience and for their previous bad behaviour. When he reached it, he was excited and angry. He opened fire. The blood flowing to his brain became congested. He may have misjudged the position, thinking that the two waves as they surged back were going to rush him. He fired at first to warn and punish; he continued firing because he feared his force might be overwhelmed. His mind became confused and he went on firing. It was already a prey to the disease which, if he had been accused of murder in the enlightened days of Lord Devlin's charge to the jury in the case of Kemp, would have freed him of legal responsibility. That is the kindest excuse we can find for Dyer.

He marched from the Jallianwala Bagh, his mind a turmoil of conflicting thoughts. He had killed hundreds of people. A naturally kind and humane man, the vision of the stricken field must have darkened his thoughts. He arrived dazed and shaken at the Ram Bagh where he found Miles Irving. He thought the Bagh had several exits, he said. He thought the crowd had turned from them to attack him. 'I never knew there was no way out', he told the Deputy Commissioner. That night and the following nights, Dyer could not sleep, seeing it all over and over again. He brooded about it, talked about it, forgot some things and exaggerated others. He had crushed the rebellion. He was a hero, he was told, and he came to see himself as other men saw him.

When he was asked for an explanation he justified himself by saying he intended that all along. He came to believe it himself because he dare not doubt it. At the Hunter Committee hearing, when he saw that his explanations were not accepted, he tried to bluff it out. Rather than reject the explanation which made him feel secure, he chose a martyr's crown.

No one but fanatical patriots could accept Dyer's explanation of his deed. The High Command in India could not stomach it; they had condoned his action on his earlier explanation. The Governments of India and Britain were forced to repudiate Dyer. They may have deprecated his clumsiness rather than his act but, on his own showing, his action was inexcusable. Political expediency may have had something to do with it; sincere distaste settled it. Dyer was lightly treated; he had no cause for complaint. But his early condonation and the long delay in bringing the matter to issue led many people to support him, not necessarily because they condoned his act, but because they felt a soldier had been shabbily treated. None the less, the support of Dyer, and his exoneration by influential people, including a learned judge, was an extraordinary expression of British public opinion.

The thousands who acclaimed Dyer as the Saviour of India were only a vociferous minority. By their acclamation of Dyer a certain class gave their support to the use of terrorism in India, and they demonstrated their belief that a European life was of greater value than an Indian's. Indians were naughty children to be punished. If they conducted themselves properly, according to British standards, they might be patted on the head; if they raised their hands against the white Sahibs they had to be killed.

THE STORY ENDS WITH MURDER

They had rebelled against British rule, murdered Britons, and Dyer had inflicted condign punishment.

Those people who supported Dyer were no more callous than he; flag wavers and ultra-patriots, they believed that Britain had been appointed by God to rule natives. A century of the *Pax Britannica* induced that belief; glorious victory over Britain's most formidable foe proved its truth. The retired majors of Cheltenham and the bloodthirsty spinsters of Pimlico were drunk with victory. Dyer became the symbol of their belief in the overwhelming might and righteousness of Britain.

The walls of the Jallianwala Bagh bear still the marks of the bullets ordered to be fired, quite unjustifiably, by General Dyer, the strong man who gave India into the keeping of a half-naked saint, the first step in the birth of a new nation. Of the future implication of that transference of power we can surmise only, but we may perhaps recall the example of the Procurator of Judaea who, by an entirely justified act, took the first step which transformed a Jewish Messiah King into a World Saviour.

BIBLIOGRAPHY

'An English Woman'	'Amritsar', Blackwoods Magazine (MCCLIV. Vol. CCVII).
Barrow, General Sir George	*The Life of General Sir Charles Carmichael Monro, Bart., G.C.S.I., G.C.M.G.*, 1931.
Callwell, Major-General Sir C. E.	*Field Marshall Sir Henry Wilson, G.C.B., D.S.O., His Life and Diaries*, 1927.
Colvin, Ian	*The Life of General Dyer*, 1929.
Disorders Inquiry Committee	Evidence (5 Volumes) 1920. Report (Hunter) 1920.
Dyer, R. E. H.	Statement to Army Council (CMD 771) 1920. *The Raiders of the Sarhad*, 1921.
Gandhi, Mahatma	*Young India*, 1919-22.
Hansard	Parliamentary Debates House of Commons 5th Series Vol. 131. House of Lords 5th Series Vol. XLI.
Horniman, B. G.	*Amritsar and Our Duty to India*, 1920.
Indian National Congress	Report of Commissioners Appointed by the Punjab Sub-Committee, 1920.
Jayakar, M. R.	*The Story of My Life*, 2 v., 1958.
Mosley, Leonard	*The Last Days of the British Raj*, 1961.
Nair, Sir C. Sankaran	*Gandhi and Anarchy*, 1922.
Nehru, Jawarhartal	*An Autobiography*, 1936.
O'Dwyer, Sir Michael	*India as I Knew It*, 1925.
Thompson, Edward	*The Reconstruction of India*, 1930. *A Letter from India*, 1932.

The correspondence between the Government of India and the Secretary of State is contained in the Hunter Report.

INDEX

Ahmedabad, Disturbances, 38, 40, 41, 42
Afghan War, 105, 106
Amritsar—
    Dyer at, 15-32, 69-98
    Disturbances, 48-69
        An Englishwoman, 57, 58, 63, 64, 65, 98
        Bal Makund, Dr, 63
        Bashir, Dr, 71
        Benjamin, Mrs Nelly, 58
        Bennett, Telegraph Master, 61
        Easdon, Mrs Isabel Mary, 58, 65
        Fauq, Dr M. A., 70, 71
        Jarman, Municipal Engineer, 53, 59, 65
        Khalsa College, Principal (Waythen), 71, 79
        Kitchlew, Dr Saif-ud-din, 48, 49, 50, 52
        Lala, Jiwan Lal C.I.D., 50, 61
        Lewis, Manager, Crown Cinema, 76
        Maqbool Mahmood, 61, 69
        Parsonage, Sergeant, 65
        Robinson, Rail guard, 61
        Ross, Assistant Manager Chartered Bank, 58, 59, 65
        Rowlands, Sergeant, 60, 65
        Satyapal, Dr, 48, 49, 50, 52
        Scott, Assistant Manager National Bank, 58
        Sherwood, Miss Marcella, 58, 65, 93, 94, 95, 96
        Smith, Lt. Colonel Henry, Civil Surgeon, 50, 51, 56, 57
        Stewart, Manager National Bank, 58
        Subedar Zardad Khan, 61
        Thompson, G. M., Manager, Alliance Bank, 58
        Thompson, J. W., Manager, Chartered Bank, 58, 59, 65
    Troops, 72, 73, 77
    Officials (Civil and Military)—
        Bechett, R. B., Assistant Commissioner, 52, 54, 55
        Botting, Captain John, 51, 61
        Bostock, Captain J. A., 71
        Briggs, Captain F. C., D.S.O., 18, 47, 69, 71, 77, 91, 106, 120, 128
        Browne, Lieutenant, 61
        Clarke, Major F. A. S., 69
        Connor, F. A., Extra Assistant Commissioner, 55
        Crampton, Captain, 61
        Dickie, Lieutenant, 55, 56
        Farquhar, C. G., Deputy Inspector of Police, 60, 63, 79, 135
        Irving, Miles, Deputy Commissioner, 24, 31, 32, 48, 49, 50, 51, 52, 54, 55, 56, 60, 61, 72, 79, 84, 87, 88, 90, 92, 169-71, 173
        Kitchin, A. J. W., Commissioner, 63, 65, 70, 71, 74, 79, 88, 89
        Kotwali (Central Police Station)
            Khan Sahib Ahmad Jan, Deputy Superintendent, 59, 60
            Muhammed Ashraf Khan, City Inspector, 59, 60, 73, 74
        MacDonald, Inspector General of Police, 90
        MacDonald, Major, 65, 68, 69
        Massey, Captain J. W. (O.C. Troops), 50, 51, 52, 53, 54, 55, 61, 63, 64
        Plomer, R., Deputy Superintendent of Police, 21, 50, 52, 54, 56, 61, 77
        Rehill, J. F., Superintendent of Police, 23, 50, 52, 74, 76, 77
        Shirley, Major S. R. (Provost Marshal), 94
    Kucha Kaurianwala (Crawling Lane), 58, 93, 94, 95, 96, 97, 99, 141
    Martial Law, 91

Barrett, General Sir Arthur (Commanding Peshawar), 106
Barrow, General Sir George, 19, 119, 120, 121, 123, 124, 128, 149-52, 161, 166, 167, 173
Beynon, General Sir William (Divisional Commander), 43, 69, 80, 84, 98, 113, 116, 118, 119, 126
Birkenhead, Earl of (Lord Chancellor), 157, 158

INDEX

Chelmsford, Lord (Viceroy), 97, 100, 112
Chirol, Sir Valentine, 161
Churchill, Rt. Hon. Winston, M.P. (later Sir), 139, 140, 153, 154, 155, 173
Colvin, Ian, 72, 76, 77, 91, 106, 107, 113, 117, 118, 119, 120, 121, 126, 127, 128, 137, 138, 164, 176
Commons, House of, Debate, 153, 154, 155
Connaught, Duke of, 161
Crewe, Marquis of, 157

Delhi, Disturbances, 36
Devlin, Lord, 164
Dyer, General R. E. H.—
    Amritsar, 15-32, 69-78, 79, 88, 89, 90, 91, 92, 93, 94, 95, 96, 97, 98, 103, 171-8
    Biographical details — Subsequent service, 113, 116-18, 128, 129, 137
    Criticisms of, 132, 133, 134, 135, 136, 139-42, 176-8
    Dalhousie, 107, 108
    Delhi, 38
    England, 138, 155, 162, 163, 164, 165, 166, 167, 168
    Explanations, 13, 17, 18, 19, 21, 22, 23, 24, 31, 32, 79, 88, 92, 93, 94, 98, 108, 109, 110, 111, 119-27, 144-9, 169-71, 174-6
    Hunter Committee, 116, 118, 119-27
    Jullundur, 47, 61, 69
    Lahore, 93
    Proclamations, 73, 74, 75
    Simla, 106

Gandhi, Mahatma, 16, 34, 35, 39, 42
Guranwala, Disturbances, 83, 84, 136
    General Campbell, 100, 101, 136

Hayat Khan, Sir Umar, 119
Herbert, Government Advocate, 96, 97, 124, 125
Hunter Committee, 17, 19, 21, 23, 24, 39, 46, 51, 53, 56, 59, 60, 62, 70, 72, 75, 76, 79, 85, 87, 93, 94, 95, 96, 99, 100, 102, 103, 105, 112, 116, 117-27, 131, 132, 135, 136, 173
Hudson, Sir Havelock (Adjutant General), 113, 114, 115, 116, 131

India, Government of, 81, 82, 83, 107, 108, 129, 132, 133, 134, 135
Irving, Miles (see Amritsar Officials)

Jallianwala Bagh—
    Massacre, 15-31
    Meaning of name, 16
    Memorial, 162
    News of, 87
    Number killed and wounded, 24, 26, 27, 28, 29, 30
Jayakar, M. R., 16, 34, 50, 56, 100

Kasur—
    Disturbances at, 46
    Captain Doveton, 101, 136
    Lieutenant Colonel Macrae, 101, 102
    Area Officer, 103
Kemp, R. V. *Kemp* (1957), 164
Kitchen, A. J. W. (see Amritsar Officials)

Lahore, Disturbances at, 38, 39, 42, 43, 44, 45
    Johnson, Colonel Frank, 45, 102, 103, 136
Lords, House of—
    Debate, 153, 155, 156, 157-60

Martial Law, 82, 91, 99-104
MacDonald, Rt. Hon. J. Ramsay, M.P., 167
McCardie, the Hon. Mr Justice (Sir Henry), 165, 166
Meston, Lord, 158, 159, 160
Monro, General Sir Charles (C.-in-C. India), 105, 106, 113, 128, 129, 130, 131, 137
Montague, Rt. Hon. E. S., Secretary of State, India, 97, 106, 107, 108, 129, 139, 140, 141, 154, 165
Morning Post, 119, 153, 156, 160, 162, 163

Nair, Sir Sankaran, 99, 129, 164, 167
Narayan, Pandit Jayat, 96, 124, 125, 132
National Congress, Sub-Committee of Inquiry, 16, 63, 93, 99, 105, 113, 136, 137

Nehru, Pandit, 34, 47, 103, 104, 127, 171, 174
Nizamabad, Disturbances, 86

O'Dwyer, Sir Michael (Lieutenant Governor, Punjab), 35, 38, 42, 43, 46, 79, 80, 81, 82, 84, 86, 87, 88, 93, 97, 105, 106, 107, 108, 116, 120, 129, 130, 134, 135, 136, 140, 142, 155, 164-5, 168
Olivier, Lord (Secretary of State, India), 167

Passive Resistance Movement, 34
Press views, 142, 143
Punjab, Disturbances, 46, 74, 83, 86

Rankin, Mr Justice (later Sir G. C.), 96
Rattigan, Sir Henry (Chief Justice, Punjab), 81
Rowlatt Acts, 34, 35, 39, 135
Rowlatt, Sir Sidney, 34

Sardar Sahibzada Sultan Ahmed Khan, 125, 132
'Satagrapha' Vow, 34
Setalvad, Sir C. H., 122, 123
Sinha, Lord (Under Secretary of State, India), 157

Tagore, Rabindranath, 161
Thompson, Edward (reporter, *Guardian*), 161, 169-71, 173

Udham Singh, 104, 168

Vincent, Sir William (Home Member, Government of India), 162

Watson (reporter of *Pioneer*), 121, 126
Whitehead, Bishop of Madras, 161
Wilson, Field-Marshal Sir H. (Chief Imperial General Staff), 139, 140

GEORGE ALLEN & UNWIN LTD
London : 40 Museum Street, W.C.1

Auckland : 24 Wyndham Street
Bombay : 15 Graham Road, Ballard Estate, Bombay 1
Buenos Aires : Escritorio 454-459, Florida 165
Calcutta : 17 Chittaranjan Avenue, Calcutta 13
Cape Town : 109 Long Street
Hong Kong : F1/12 Mirador Mansions, Kowloon
Ibadan : P.O. Box 62
Karachi : Karachi Chambers, McLeod Road
Madras : Mohan Mansions, 38c Mount Road, Madras 6
Mexico : Villalongin 32-10, Piso, Mexico 5, D.F.
Nairobi : P.O. Box 4536
New Delhi : 13-14 Asaf-Ali Road, New Delhi 1
São Paulo : Avenida 9 De Julho 1138-Ap. 51
Singapore : 36c Prinsep Street, Singapore 7
Sydney, N.S.W. : Bradbury House, 55 York Street
Tokyo : 3 Kanda-Ogawamachi, 3-Chome, Chiyoda-Ku
Toronto : 91 Wellington Street West, Toronto 1

For Product Safety Concerns and Information please contact our EU
representative GPSR@taylorandfrancis.com
Taylor & Francis Verlag GmbH, Kaufingerstraße 24, 80331 München, Germany

www.ingramcontent.com/pod-product-compliance
Lightning Source LLC
Chambersburg PA
CBHW061834300426
44115CB00013B/2372